To Dad.
  Many happy returns, 5/9/98.
From William.

Military Blunders II

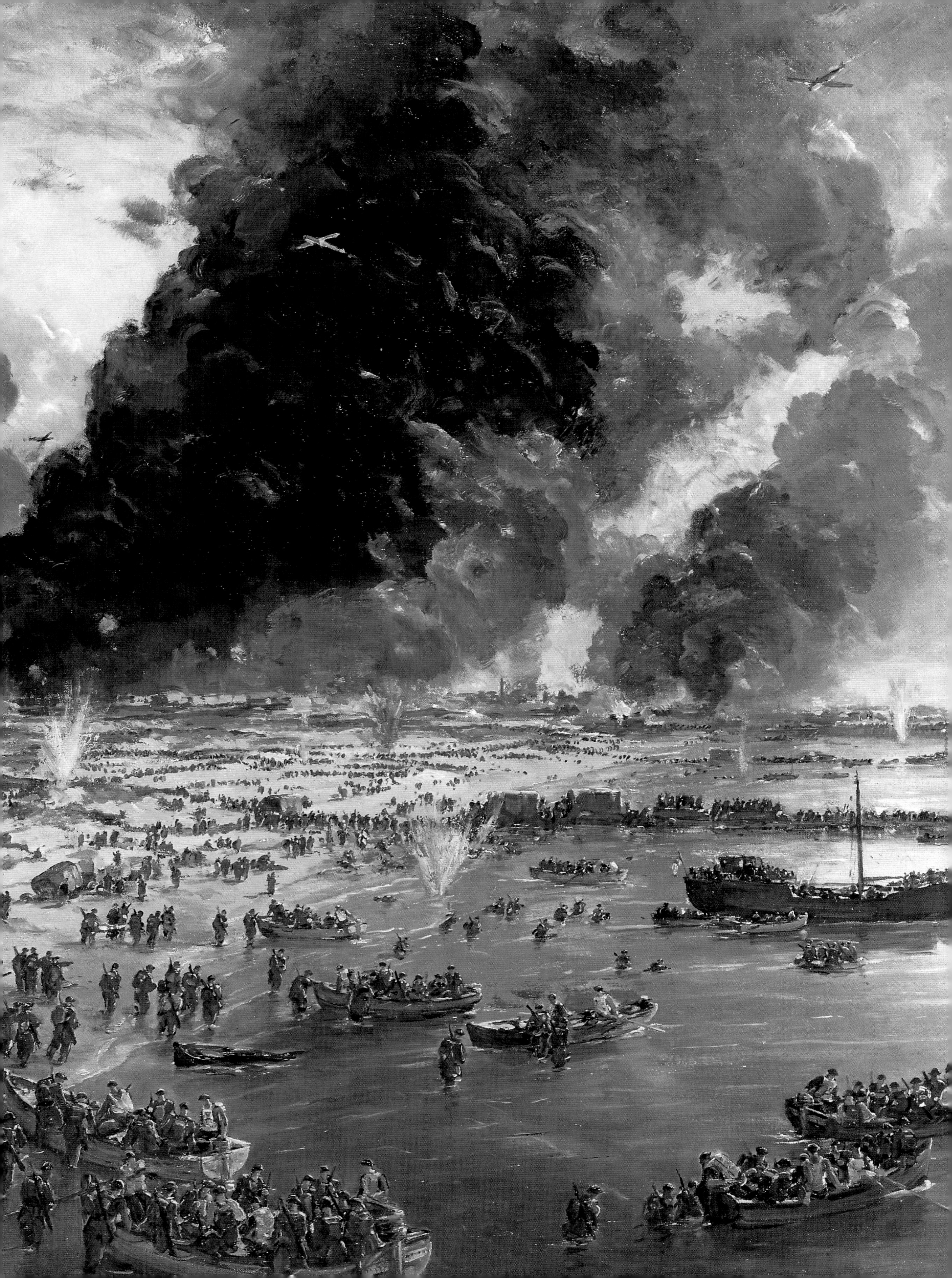

Military Blunders II

The Twentieth Century

Major Steven Eden, U.S. Army

MetroBooks

To Kathleen—for her support and love

MetroBooks

An Imprint of Friedman/Fairfax Publishers

© 1996 by Michael Friedman Publishing Group, Inc.

Library of Congress Cataloging-in-Publication data available upon request.

ISBN 1-56799-388-5

Editor: Benjamin Boyington
Art Director: Lynne Yeamans
Photography Editor: Emilya Naymark

Color separations by Ocean Graphic International Company Ltd.
Printed in China by Leefung Asco Printers Ltd.

For bulk purchases and special sales, please contact:
Friedman/Fairfax Publishers
Attention: Sales Department
15 West 26th Street
New York, NY 10010
212/685-6610 FAX 212/685-1307

Visit the Friedman/Fairfax Website:
http://www.webcom.com/friedman

Contents

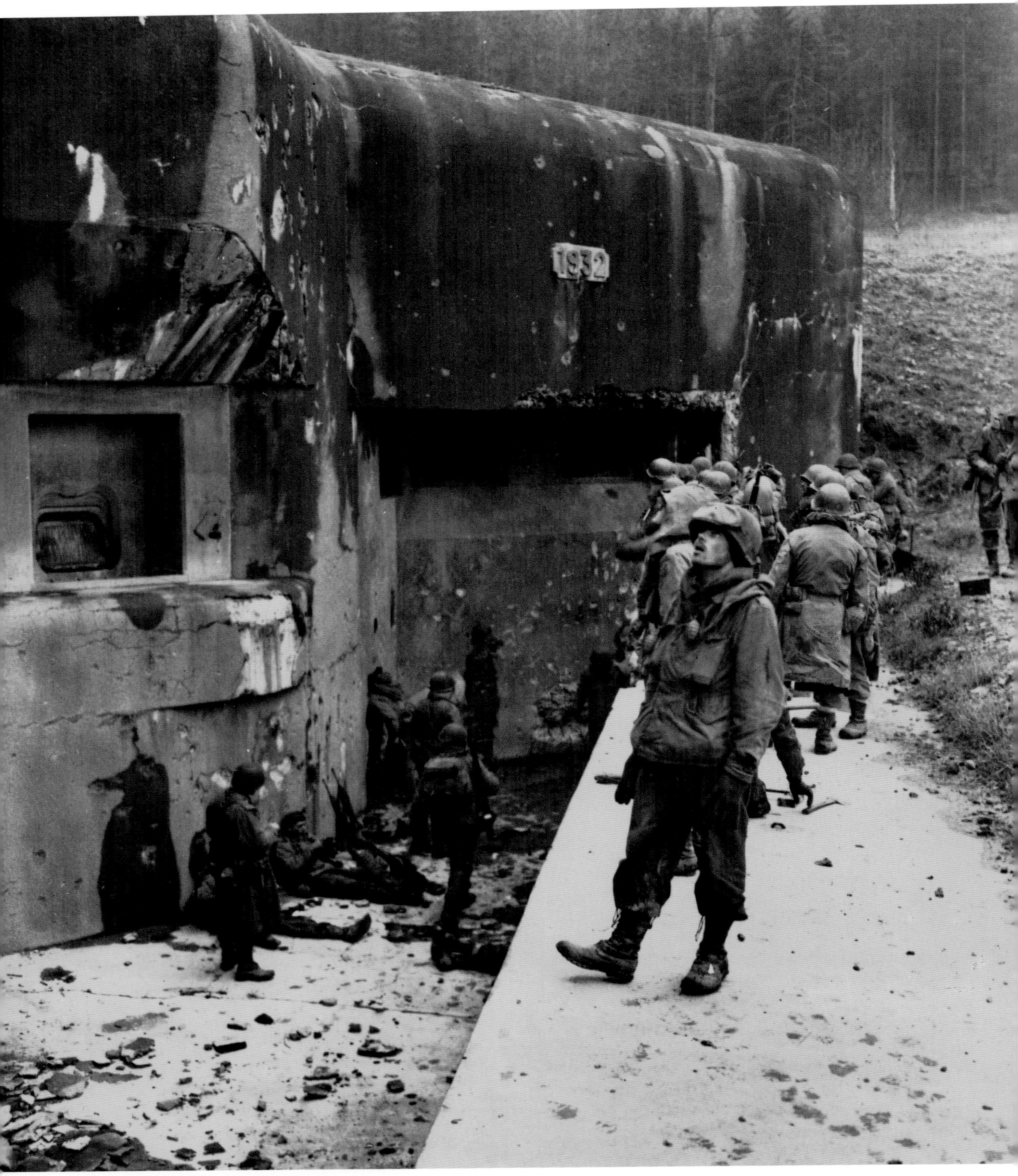
1932

Introduction

Where Lies the Blame?

They stand silent vigil now over peaceful fields and woodland, knobs of steel and concrete rising incongruously out of the earth. Empty apertures gape where powerful cannon once stood, guarding the French border against German invasion. But the turrets of the Maginot Line are merely the visible tip of an amazing underground complex built in the late 1920s and early thirties to defend a France determined to avoid repeating the bloodbath of World War I. Beneath the turrets, pillboxes, and cupolas on the surface were air-conditioned barracks, magazines, mess halls, hospitals, gymnasiums, and power plants. Tanks and planes stood ready in underground motor pools and hangars, while subway trains and buried telephone lines connected the separate forts of the Line. Tank traps and barbed wire guarded the approaches to the Line, and anti-aircraft guns stood ready to repel bombers. For 87 miles (139.2km), from the Swiss border, along the Rhenish frontier, and into the rugged foothills of the Ardennes, the Maginot Line blocked the most likely invasion routes. It was a magnificent breastwork: modern, immensely strong, cleverly sited—and utterly useless. In fact, it was worse than useless. Construction of the world's strongest defensive position doomed France to humiliating defeat.

When war finally came in 1939, France initially enjoyed an overwhelming numerical advantage in the west. It took the Germans just over a month to dispatch Poland. Unwilling to abandon the imagined strength of the Line, however, the French let this opportunity pass with only a few timid jabs at Germany's weak western flank. When the Germans unleashed the blitzkrieg against the French and their British, Dutch, and Belgian allies in 1940, they simply outflanked the Maginot Line, roaring through the supposedly impassable Ardennes forest and piercing the Allied front at its weakest point, near Sedan on the Meuse River. Within ten days, the panzers had reached the English Channel, trapping the bulk of the British Expeditionary Force and much of the French Army with their backs to the sea; a month later, France had capitulated and the English had retreated back to their island fortress, leaving the Germans masters of Europe. The garrisons of the Maginot Line forts, meanwhile, had scarcely fired a shot.

The Maginot Line remains a monument to military incompetence, but incompetence of a very modern sort. Its designers were not stupid men, but they possessed a limited imagination. They understood the power of modern weapons such as the plane and tank (in 1940, the French boasted more and better armored vehicles than the Germans), but they failed to see the potential of these weapons when combined with wireless communications and the truck. They still believed that huge, fixed fortifications would play a significant role in future wars. They even anticipated a German thrust

American soldiers sight-see along the Maginot Line in 1944. The long-abandoned casements remain impressive.

The visible domes and turrets of the Maginot Line concealed a labyrinthine underground world of magazines, barracks, hospitals, and more.

around the open end of the Line, and therefore deployed the greater part of their mobile forces into Belgium to forestall it.

Unfortunately, the cost of the Maginot Line (estimated at close to 80 million francs per mile [1.6km]) hamstrung French efforts to build an army capable of fending off the Nazi juggernaut. If directed elsewhere, these resources might have purchased two dozen armored divisions (the Germans attacked with only ten), forty additional infantry divisions, 10,000 fighter aircraft, or 3,000 medium bombers. Of course, there is no guarantee that the châteaux-bound French generals would have employed these extra forces any more competently, but they could have addressed their two foremost weaknesses: the lack of a strong, mobile reserve and of an air force capable of disputing mastery of the air with the German Luftwaffe. The immense investment poured into the Maginot Line produced few dividends in wartime.

And this is what makes the construction of the Maginot Line such a sublime example of the modern military blunder. In an era of total war, the wise investment of resources and the prescience of military thinkers during peacetime can have as much effect on the outcome of a campaign as the ability of the field general once action begins. The French government and its military bureaucracy guessed wrongly, losing their army and independence as a result. In this book we shall examine other examples of "wrong guesses" about the nature of future wars and the subsequent disasters they wrought, such as the holocaust of merchant shipping engendered by bureaucratic infighting during Operation Drumbeat in 1942; the misdirected sledgehammer blows of the Rolling Thunder air campaign in the Vietnam War; or that war's turning point on the ground, the Tet Offensive of 1968.

The twentieth century has also introduced completely new forms of warfare in the air and at sea. The advent of true strategic bombing presented planners with knotty problems of how best to apply their strength from the air

does one blame? Both the Rangers at Pointe-du-Hoe on D-Day and the Son Tay raiders during the Vietnam War executed their assignments with great elan, but both came up empty-handed, victims of some nameless staff officer. The American hostage rescue attempt in Iran and the massive raid against Dieppe in World War II each failed, the victims of unworkable or flawed plans—but try as one might, it is difficult to peel back the layers of the bureaucratic onion and find out how or why these plans came into being in the first place.

Somehow, this is much more chilling than simple military idiocy.

against the enemy's homeland, problems that had to be solved by trial and error as there was precious little experience to fall back on. Some of the errors proved extremely costly, such as Göring's last-minute blunder during the Battle of Britain, which saved England from German defeat, or the disastrous attacks against Schweinfurt and Ploesti by American bombers in 1943.

Another novel form of warfare involved the first sea battles in which neither fleet actually saw the other—all attacks were made by land-based or carrier-borne aircraft. The classic example is the Battle of Midway, in which five minutes of combat literally changed the course of World War II in the Pacific. Across the globe, at roughly the same time, Nazi bombers and submarines were ravaging the ships of Convoy PQ-17, a formation whose fate rested in the hands of a man who couldn't even see his own fleet.

Of course, the century still provided ample scope for the good old-fashioned military blunder: Hitler's mad obsession with Stalingrad, which cost him an army and a war; Spanish and French hubris at Anual and Dien Bien Phu, respectively, against badly underestimated colonial foes; the normally brilliant MacArthur's overconfidence in Korea, which led to the longest retreat

ever conducted by an American army; and the massacre of Russian soldiers at Suomussalmi in 1940 by a handful of hardy Finns.

As we approach the twenty-first century, though, it is getting harder to assign blame for disaster. Modern war, like modern business or government, is increasingly run by committees. Legions of planners, each with his or her own special area of expertise, produce schemes that are executed by others. When things go wrong, who, exactly,

Top: Had it not been for the courage and resourcefulness of the Royal Air Force, the Allies probably would have lost World War II. The mainstay of the RAF pilots was the Spitfire fighter plane. Above: MacArthur followed his most brilliant strategic stroke, the Inchon landing (shown here), with his most ill-considered maneuver: the risky, hasty rush to the Yalu.

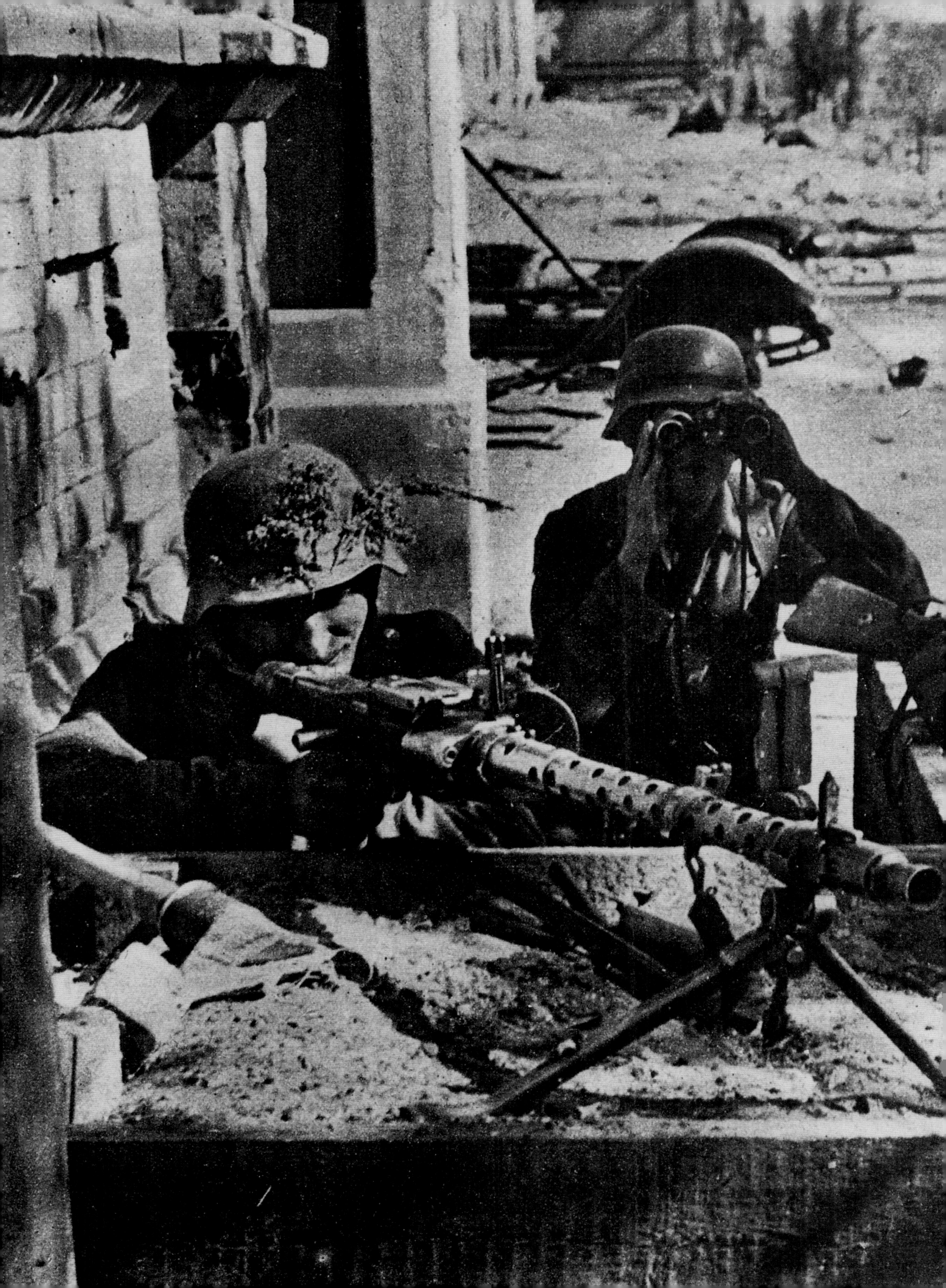

1

SUOMUSSALMI • STALINGRAD
CH'ONGCH'ON RIVER AND
CHOSIN RESERVOIR • GOLAN HEIGHTS

Land Warfare

Land war underwent a metamorphosis in the twentieth century. Machine power replaced muscle power in propelling armies across the battlefield. Rates of advance, once tied to the speed of footsore infantry or horses, multiplied with the introduction of the internal combustion engine. The truck and the tank broke the trench deadlock that frustrated both sides during World War I, freeing armies to maneuver. At the same time, though, advances in radio communication gave commanders greater control of their forces, allowing coordination of men and machines despite distance or terrain.

These technological advances facilitated campaigns marked by a speed and decisiveness not seen since the days of Napoleon. While armies had grown too large to be destroyed in a single afternoon, they could be defeated in a comparatively short time. In World War II, the French were overrun in six weeks, the Poles in less than a month, and the Dutch and Belgians in a matter of days. In six days in 1967, the Israelis annihilated the Egyptian army; more recently, the Iraqis were defeated by the U.S.-led alliance in less than 100 hours.

But the quickened tempo and enlarged geographical scope of war have not invalidated its basic principles, formulated by thousands of years of conflict. Those who have violated the laws of war have still done so at their own risk. Nor has the advent of the tank and the motor-

ization of armies proved an unmixed blessing. Many armies have become dependent on mobility or firepower and have stumbled badly when unable to use one or the other. Moreover, a modern army's constant need for supplies and spare parts has led to vulnerabilities whenever its supply lines have come under attack.

Consider one of the classic blunders of this century. In November 1939, the mighty Soviet Union attacked tiny Finland. Suprisingly, the Soviets, facing an army equipped with little more than small arms and brute courage, suffered a series of humiliating reverses, the worst of which occurred near a tiny logging village just south of the Arctic Circle.

The Russian plan was simple: while forces in the north overran the Finnish port of Petsamo and southern armies broke through the Mannerheim Line to Helsinki, the Soviet Union's Ninth Army would complete the conquest by cutting Finland in half at its narrowest point. The Ninth Army's ultimate objective was the capture of the Gulf of Bothnia and the port of Oulu, but to get there it would have to fight through miles of virgin forest in winter. With overwhelming advantages in aircraft, tanks, artillery, and manpower, the Soviets were confident. But they soon discovered the consequences of waging modern warfare in primitive terrain with troops, commanders, and equipment that were ill-prepared for an Arctic battlefield.

German panzer grenadiers scan for snipers in Stalingrad in 1942.

Suomussalmi

No, the Finnish woods are altogether unlike our Ukraine.

—From a diary entry of a slain Russian officer

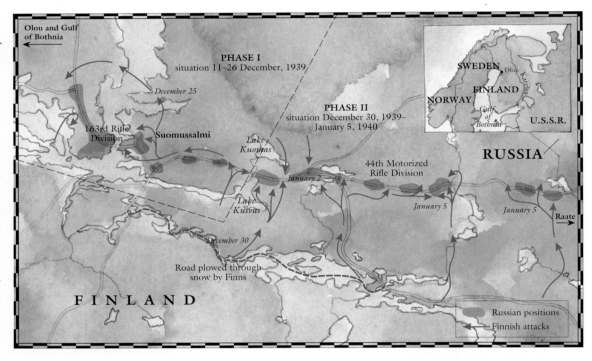

On the last day of November 1939, 100 miles (160km) below the Arctic Circle, shivering troops of the Soviet Union's 163rd Rifle Division plunged into the dark woods of Finnish Karelia. Brushing aside small detachments of border guards, the 163rd entered a pristine wilderness of endless forest dotted with rivers, frozen swamps, and lakes. Only two narrow roads wound their way from the border to the west, intersecting at the lakeside village of Suomussalmi some 20 miles (32km) inside Finland. Despite poor trafficability, tenaciously defended roadblocks, and constant harassment by Finnish patrols, the 163rd, commanded by Major General Zelentsov, ground ahead steadily, reaching Suomussalmi on December 7. Only a scratch force of Finns—lacking any tanks, artillery, or antitank guns—barred the way to Oulu and the Gulf of Bothnia.

Several factors conspired to bring the Russian advance to a halt: the temperature plunged to an incredible –40 degrees Fahrenheit (–40°C), and the Soviet soldiers, most of them recently conscripted from the vast plains of the Ukraine, were ill-equipped to deal with the numbing cold. Similarly, they lacked any experience in fighting among the thick coniferous forests of central Finland. Finally, the winter's heavy snowfalls left the Soviet column virtually roadbound and unable to bring their considerable manpower advantage to bear at any one place.

Above: The secret of the Finns' success was their ability to traverse the trackless forests of Karelia, while the Russians were bound to the few miserable roads.

The Finns, however, were operating in their own element. Most of the defenders were local men, familiar with the terrain and wise in the ways of forest fighting. Many Finnish units routinely traveled over the loose snowdrifts on skis, and they either dragged their heavy equipment behind them on sledges or plowed makeshift roads for their few trucks on the terrain's numerous frozen waterways. The hardy Finns also possessed excellent cold-weather gear, including tents, camp stoves, and even mobile saunas, which allowed them to pass the frigid nights comfortably while their Russian counterparts huddled miserably around open fires.

At the beginning of December, Colonel Hjalmar Siilasvuo, a tough veteran of World War I, arrived to take charge of all Finnish forces operating near Suomussalmi. On the eleventh of the month, he ordered a counterattack against the stalled 163rd. Moving wraithlike through the forest in their white camouflage parkas, Finnish ski troops cut the roads leading back to the border and then broke the strung-out Russian column into several isolated pockets, or *mottis* (Finnish for stacks of wood that are ready for chopping). The Soviets, unable to do more than flounder a few hundred yards into the snow-packed woods, vainly attempted to reopen their supply lifeline on the gloomy road to Raate, only to be turned back. Constant Finnish probes confused Zelentsov—the enemy seemed to be everywhere, emerging suddenly from the forest to cut the road or ambush an unwary unit, only to vanish again. Soviet

Above: Lightly armed Finnish ski troops move through the Karelian woods. Left: Ill-clad Russian troops taken prisoner near Suomussalmi. Note the blackened, frozen hands of the soldier on the left.

The Finns were armed and equipped by their German allies, although often what they got was hand-me-down gear. Note the thickness of the Karelian woods.

tanks, when they could be started in the subzero temperatures, proved useless in the thickly wooded terrain, unable to move off the road or fire through the trees.

Within a week, the 163rd was completely surrounded, its soldiers demoralized by hunger, cold, and the seeming invincibility of the Finns. The Finns, meanwhile, continued to probe the surviving elements, seeking to break up the mottis into smaller packets, and overrunning each in turn as it was reduced to a manageable size. In some places, the terrified Soviets fled into the woods at the first Finn approach, doomed to freeze or be hunted down. In other areas, the Soviets grimly held their ground in abandoned villages or hastily constructed dugouts, supported by tanks along their perimeter; short of manpower, the Finns left these mottis to the winter's cold embrace.

Meanwhile, reinforcements for both sides poured into the region. By Christmas Eve, the Finns had assembled three infantry regiments, along with some desperately needed artillery and anti-tank guns. Designated the 9th Division, this force contained some 12,000 men, by no means enough to make Colonel Siilasvuo comfortable about his prospects. He faced sizable remnants of the 163rd that were still hunkered down around Suomussalmi, and now the 44th Motorized Rifle Division, a veteran unit led by one General Vinogradov, was rapidly approaching along the road from Raate.

On December 24, the Finns faced their sternest challenge. The 163rd made an all-out attempt to break free of their tormentors while the lead elements of the 44th Division massed against the outer ring of the encirclement. The attacks continued throughout Christmas

Arctic Warfare

Fighting in the extreme cold takes special training and equipment—a truism one would think the Soviets would have learned long before 1939. But the soldiers who invaded Finland in the depth of the Arctic winter had neither.

Soviet tanks and weapons often malfunctioned because their lubricants turned gummy in the intense cold; moreover, drivers had not been taught to run their vehicles for a few minutes every hour or so to prevent the engine from freezing solid. Drugs and plasma likewise froze when inexperienced medics failed to safeguard them against the harsh temperatures. The soldiers lacked energy, as their meager rations did not supply the extra calories necessary for cold-weather operations.

Nor were the soldiers prepared to fight in snow. Their uniforms and vehicles were gray, which made them stand out against the white background. Few Soviet infantrymen had skis; those who did had not been trained to use them in combat and so could not trail the elusive Finns when they chose to fade back into the forest.

Finally, the Soviet army had few tools with which to provide warmth for the men, which is not a luxury but a matter of survival in Arctic warfare. Without camp stoves, the soldiers were forced to rely on open fires for heat, which immediately attracted Finnish mortar and sniper fire. Large field kitchens provided the sole source of hot food, but these were difficult to camouflage; the wily Finns made a point of singling them out, ultimately destroying every single kitchen that belonged to the 44th Division.

The Finnish winter proved to be as deadly a foe as the Finns themselves. One in ten Soviet soldiers was a frostbite casualty before the troops even crossed the border, and the apathetic showing of many Soviet units around Suomussalmi undoubtedly reflected the draining effort needed to fight the constant, numbing cold.

Day, backed by incessant air strikes and heavy artillery bombardment, which severely strained the Finnish resources. While the Finns surrounding the stranded soldiers held on by the skin of their teeth, Siilasvuo watched with trepidation as Vinogradov prepared to hammer the only obstacle between them and the 163rd: a roadblock erected between Lakes Kuivas and Kuomas, held by a weak Finnish infantry battalion and a handful of antitank guns.

Luckily for the Finns, Vinogradov lost his nerve at this critical juncture. As he peered into the primeval woodlands and listened to the increasingly frantic calls for help from Zelentsov, Vinogradov imagined a much larger enemy force than what actually lay before him. After a few halfhearted attempts to break through, the Soviet commander called off the attacks, though in reality the Finns were themselves nearing defeat. As Christmas Day drew to a close, the 163rd found itself exhausted and critically short of supplies. The fighting died away over the next two days, as Vinogradov attempted to summon his courage and Siilasvuo's troops moved in for the kill.

Beginning on December 27, the 9th Division launched several concerted assaults against the 163rd. Over the next two days, the fragmented Soviet division was annihilated while Vinogradov and his forces dithered only six miles (9.6km) away. Only a few survivors managed to escape eastward; Zelentsov was not among them.

Siilasvuo now turned his attention to the 44th Division. Vinogradov, having failed to rescue the 163rd, now faced destruction himself. His unit was stretched out along—and limited to—nearly 15 miles (24km) of inadequate road hemmed in by thick forest, along which the nimble Finns could target an attack at any point from north or south. In other words, his position mirrored that of Zelentsov's just a few weeks before. Merely digging in and awaiting the Finns would be to adopt the same tactic that had doomed the 163rd Division, but this was precisely what the panicked Vinogradov proceeded to do.

As the Soviet forces futilely scratched shallow trenches in the frozen earth and felled trees along either side of the road, Siilasvuo's tired soldiers redeployed against their next victim. On New Year's Day of 1940, the attacks began: the 44th Division was systematically broken up into several mottis, the bulk of the Finnish forces descending on the weak spots while one detachment cut the road east of the 44th, blocking reinforcements from the Soviet Union. Desperate Soviet tank attacks to reopen the road only piled flaming wrecks in front of roadblocks, further strengthening the Finnish positions. Hungry, dispirited, and nearly frozen, the Soviets could do little to stop the Finnish onslaught. By January 6, as Vinogradov watched one motti after another surrender or dissolve in flight to the east, the Russian commander finally authorized those who could still escape to try to do so. But it was too late—on January 8, the last organized resistance ended, and the 44th Motorized Rifle Division was reduced to a few fugitive bands stumbling blindly through the Karelian forest.

Within a month of the initial Finnish counterattack, the Soviet Union had lost two entire divisions at Suomussalmi. Though an embarrassed Soviet army has never released a final count, at least 22,000 Soviet soldiers were killed, wounded, or captured by an enemy that amounted to barely half that number. Additionally, the Finns captured forty-three tanks, seventy field guns, and hundreds of trucks, tractors, and armored cars. The Finns themselves lost approximately 2,700 men. As for Vinogradov, the hapless commander escaped the carnage in one of his few remaining tanks—only to be court-martialed and shot a few days later by the NKVD, the forerunner of the KGB.

✦ ✦ ✦

The Soviet Union had blundered by sending unprepared troops into the Karelian winter wilderness and trying to use motorized forces in a nearly trackless environment—decisions that became fatal because of the passivity of commanders facing the almost instinctual fighting excellence of the Finnish defenders. In other words, Suomussalmi became a classic example of the disastrous consequences of fighting an enemy on its own turf.

Of course, the Russo-Finnish War was a sideshow, quickly eclipsed by the titanic struggle that ensued eighteen months later between Nazi Germany and the Soviet Union. When Adolf Hitler, flush with recent victories over France and a host of lesser enemies, invaded the Soviet Union in June 1941, he thought it would be the final act of World War II. Instead, he initiated the greatest land campaign in history, a sweeping war of millions that would dwarf the action at Suomussalmi. Despite the conflict's mammoth scale, Hitler proved that one man could still decisively influence an outcome—if only the magnitude of his blunders was great enough.

The Finns' primitive transport actually served them better in the deep snow than did the modern trucks and tanks of the Soviets.

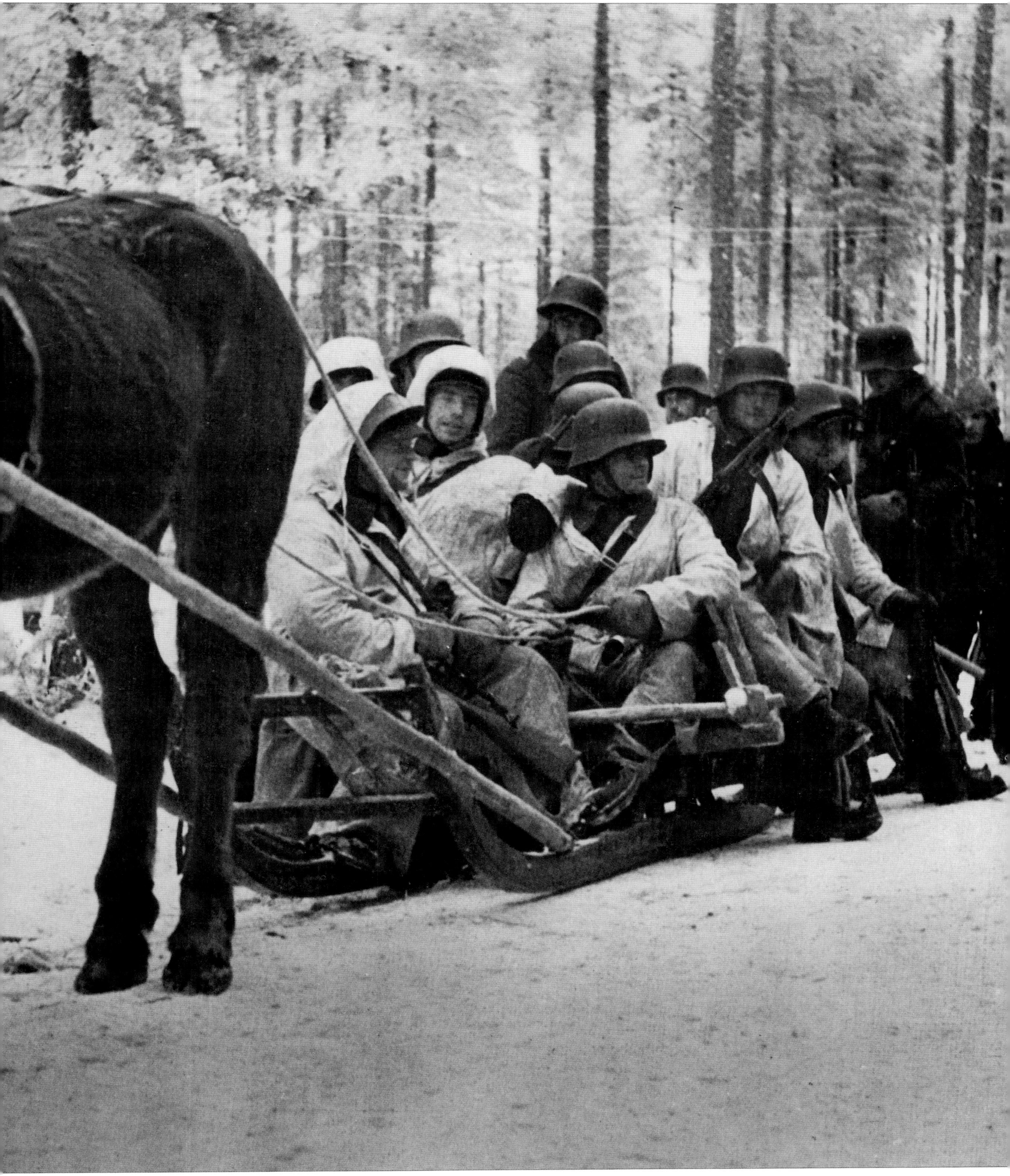

Stalingrad

Long live the Führer! Long live Germany!

—The last message sent from Stalingrad

The speedy victory that Hitler had expected in the summer of 1941 eluded him. His armored blitz petered out within sight of the Kremlin spires, and the Germans spent a brutal winter deep within the Soviet Union. As the snows melted in the spring of 1942, the Nazis and their allies gathered strength for a summer campaign that they hoped would force the Soviet Union out of the war. Hitler and his generals realized that a general offensive across the entire eastern front was out of the question, given the reduced strength of the Wehrmacht. They opted instead for an attack in southern Russia to capture the Caucasus oil fields; the northern and central sectors would remain static.

The original plan envisaged a phased operation. In the first phase, Field Marshal Fedor von Bock's Army Group South would drive eastward to destroy all Soviet forces west of the Don River from Voronezh southward; Army Group South would then be split into Army Groups A and B. Thus would begin the second phase: von Bock, retaining control of Army Group B, would establish a solid front along the Don and Volga Rivers, using the city of Stalingrad as its southern anchor. Army Group A, commanded by Field Marshal Wilhelm List, would simultaneously seize Rostov and the crossings over the southern Don. Only when Army Group B had secured List's flank and rear

Top: Field Marshal Fedor von Bock became a scapegoat for the failures of the 1942 German offensive in Russia. Above: Hitler's thrust into southern Russia left his forces terribly overstretched and exhausted by his insane fixation on capturing the city named after his nemesis.

would the final phase begin: the drive to the Caucasus and its vital oil fields. The loss of her oil-producing regions (and a great part of her richest agricultural land) would cripple the Soviet Union's war-making capacity, and might even lead to a negotiated peace.

The offensive opened on June 28. Army Group South attacked with 1.3 million men in ninety divisions, including twenty-five Hungarian, Italian, and Romanian divisions of dubious worth. Eleven panzer and four motorized divisions, concentrated in the First and Fourth Panzer Armies, formed the Germans' main offensive punch. Army

Group South rapidly smashed through the Soviet defenses, its armored spearheads racing across the flat Russian steppes. Voronezh fell easily on July 6; by the ninth, Army Group South was already two weeks ahead of schedule as Soviet resistance evaporated.

But there were disquieting signs. The pace of the advance had been due as much to Soviet withdrawals as to any tactical successes on the German side. The Soviets were not going to allow themselves to be surrounded as they had the previous summer—rather than stand and fight, Soviet divisions were streaming away to the northeast, east, and south, trading space for time. The German armored pincers closed again and again on empty space, and the first two weeks of the offensive bagged only 80,000 prisoners. Compared with the huge numbers captured in 1941, this was a paltry prize, and Hitler grew increasingly restive. Moreover, the deep lunges into Russian territory strained the German supply system beyond its capacity, leaving panzer divisions stranded for days days at a time because of lack of fuel.

All this led to the first of Hitler's blunders during the campaign. He accelerated the timetable for the attack south, activating Army Group A early, while removing von Bock from his command on July 12 for his failure to destroy the Soviets west of the Don. Colonel-General Maximilian von Weichs

Hitler's mania for control exploded during the fight for Stalingrad.

took over Army Group B and was promptly stripped of his panzer divisions, which were diverted to support List's attack over the southern Don. By opening the drive on the Caucasus prematurely, Hitler missed a chance to take Stalingrad on the run in late July—the Soviets had only a handful of divisions to oppose the German advance in that sector. They could not have held long against the onrushing panzers, but they did sufficiently slow the plodding German infantry to allow defenses to organize around the city.

Over the next two weeks, Hitler seemed to have realized his mistake, but his solution only made matters worse. On July 25, he issued the fateful Directive No. 45, which ordered the concurrent seizure of the Caucasus and Stalingrad. The Fourth Panzer Army was to be transferred back to Army Group B for the attack on Stalingrad.

Directive No. 45 violated several principles of war: it established two objectives; it forced the two German Army Groups to attack at right angles to each other, making mutual support impossible; and worst of all, it split the panzer armies apart, weakening each Army Group to the point where neither had enough striking power to accomplish its mission. Furthermore, it completely overloaded the supply system, now requiring it to support two major diverging offensives.

The results were predictable. With both attacks hamstrung, both fell just short of their objectives. By the middle of August, Army Group A had penetrated into, but could not fight its way through, the Caucasus Mountains. And

in early September, Army Group B had two armies poised on the outskirts of Stalingrad, prepared to take the city: the Fourth Panzer Army attacked from the south, and the Sixth Army, commanded by Colonel-General Friedrich Paulus, pushed directly into Stalingrad from the west and northwest.

For a month, the Germans battered the city, feeding division after division into the fight, but the Soviets had put to good use the short respite offered them earlier that summer. The city, stretching 12 miles (19.2km) along the west bank of the Volga River, had been turned

into a nest of fortified houses, barricaded streets, and factory strong points. After advancing nearly 300 miles (480km) in just over sixty days, the Germans now measured their daily progress in terms of blocks, if not single buildings. Casualties soared in the murderous house-to-house struggle. On October 6, with his average infantry battalion reduced to seventy men and perhaps a third of the city still in Soviet hands, Paulus called off the attack.

At this point, Hitler would have been wise to go on the defensive in the Stalingrad area. For all practical military

Luckier than their comrades trapped in Stalingrad, these German artillerymen snatch a hasty meal as they retreat east across the frozen steppes in late 1942.

purposes, the city was useless to both sides. Beyond that, occupying the remainder of the city still held by the Soviets would be hugely expensive and would not improve the position of Army Group B. As an added incentive to leave Stalingrad, German intelligence reported that significant Soviet reserves were forming farther east for a possible winter offensive. This was of special concern, considering that long stretches of

Army Group B's front had been assigned to the ineffectual Hungarian, Italian, and Romanian troops as more and more German units were shoved into the Stalingrad meat grinder.

But Hitler adamantly persisted in his orders to take the city. He saw the struggle for Stalingrad as a test of will, as a symbol of victory or defeat that transcended mere military considerations—the one remaining goal of a

failed offensive that still lay within his grasp. Consequently, the long, dreary battle continued through the fall, drawing German manpower inexorably from other fighting fronts and draining the few reserves that remained.

By November 19, the Sixth Army had taken 95 percent of the city, but that would be the extent of the German advance. That morning, an avalanche of Soviet armor pounded through the lightly armed Romanian divisions holding the lines north and south of the city. The Russian counteroffensive, carried out by more than 100 divisions that had been carefully hoarded throughout the bitter fighting of summer and fall, tore huge holes in the Romanian lines. On November 23, the southern and northern armies came together, trapping the Sixth Army and half of the Fourth Panzer Army in and around Stalingrad.

A lingering remnant of World War I strategies—trench warfare during the Battle of Stalingrad.

Kursk

While the Battle of Stalingrad ensured that the Germans could not win World War II, the Battle of Kursk ensured that they would lose it. After Stalingrad, Herculean efforts on the part of the Wehrmacht and the brilliant generalship of Field Marshal Erich von Manstein (regarded as the premier armor leader of the war) finally halted the Russian winter offensive. Von Manstein even managed to deal a stunning blow to the Soviet spearheads and regain some of the ground lost since November 1942. By March 1943, a continuous front had been patched together, and a lull fell over the east.

With an imminent Allied invasion of Italy, a greater assault against France on the horizon, and his allies rapidly losing their enthusiasm for the war, Hitler would have been well advised to move to the defensive in Russia throughout 1943. Instead, unwilling to admit that the initiative had slipped from Germany's fingers, he ordered an attack to cut out a huge salient in the German lines centered on the Ukrainian city of Kursk. Von Manstein warned that the offensive must occur before the Russians could dig in, but Hitler kept delaying the starting date in order to rebuild the panzer forces that had been so badly depleted over the winter. The dictator, fascinated by weaponry, also wanted to wait until sufficient numbers of the new Panther and Elefant tanks were on hand.

While Hitler dragged his feet, the Soviets constructed defensive lines seven miles (11.2km) deep, covered by thousands of antitank guns and millions of mines, and concentrated their own massive armor forces just behind the Kursk salient.

On July 4, despite evidence that the Soviets were ready and waiting, the attack finally began. It was a disaster. After three weeks of bitter struggle, the Germans had lost 100,000 men and more than 1,000 tanks, and had penetrated a mere 12 miles (19.2km). A Russian counterstroke broke open the front and forced the Wehrmacht back hundreds of miles across the Ukraine. The panzer force, so laboriously rebuilt after Stalingrad, would never recover from the ordeal.

Hitler had predicted that the Battle of Kursk would decide the war. He was right.

Almost as soon as the extent of the Soviet offensive became apparent, Paulus began to badger Weichs for permission to withdraw. He saw no purpose in hanging on to the worthless rubble of Stalingrad; at the same time, if the 250,000 Germans trapped there were to be saved, he had to fight his way through the encirclement before the tenuous enemy ring hardened into a band of iron.

On November 24, however, Hitler capped his mishandling of the campaign by decreeing that Stalingrad must be held: there would be no retreat. Despite serious objections by his generals, Hitler pinned his hopes on a counterattack to reopen supply lines into the city; should that fail, he claimed that troops could be supplied by air throughout the winter and relieved in the spring. Neither scheme worked. The puny forces available for a relief effort were inadequate in the face of an unraveling front, and it was only with the greatest of efforts that Army Group A was extricated from the Caucasus. Meanwhile, hundreds of transport aircraft were lost in an abortive attempt to keep the Stalingrad garrison alive.

By the middle of December, seven Soviet armies and some 2,000 guns were hammering away at the Stalingrad pocket, while further offensives had scattered Germany's allied armies and her minuscule reserves. The pocket slowly collapsed under the weight of repeated attacks until, by late January, only a few isolated diehards held out amid the ruins. On January 31, 1943, Paulus

Disease, hunger, cold, and generally brutal conditions doomed most of the Germans taken prisoner at Stalingrad.

*The staunch defense of Stalingrad forged a
new Red Army and turned the tide of World
War II in Europe.*

surrendered at last, along with his staff. Two days later, the last Germans in the city laid down their arms.

Hitler's blunders early in the summer had doomed the campaign to failure, but it was his fixation on gaining control of 12 square miles (31.2 sq km) of bombed-out rubble that brought about utter disaster. During the long autumn struggle for Stalingrad, the German dictator gradually lost touch with reality, ignoring the warning signs of the impending Soviet counteroffensive and the perilously stretched condition of his flanks. Once the blow fell, Hitler clung to desperate fantasies rather than admitting defeat and saving what he could. Consequently, twenty German divisions were destroyed in the Stalingrad pocket. Their equipment alone represented six months of war production. Of the 250,000 men trapped in Stalingrad, 30,000 wounded were evacuated by air, 147,000 died, and the remainder trudged off into captivity. Only 5,000 lived to see Germany again. Hungary, Italy, and Romania—Germany's eastern-front allies—suffered another 450,000 casualties in the Soviet counteroffensive. While communist losses could not be fully discounted (though figures were never released by the secretive Red Army), the balance of power had indeed shifted permanently in favor of the Soviets.

◆ ◆ ◆

Of course, one need not be a mad dictator to blind oneself to impending disaster. Many a fine commander has overlooked what, in hindsight, seemed to be glaringly obvious precursors of defeat. In fact, one of the twentieth century's most brilliant (albeit inconsistent) strategists managed to transform triumphant victory into panicked rout virtually overnight through a combination of willful ignorance and wishful thinking.

Ch'ongch'on River and Chosin Reservoir

We face an entirely new war.

—General Douglas MacArthur

When General of the Army Douglas MacArthur boarded a plane for his Tokyo headquarters on November 24, 1950, he thought that the war in Korea was winding down to a satisfactory conclusion. That morning, he had watched the launching of the final United Nations offensive, designed to drive to the Yalu River (the border between China and North Korea) and destroy the scattered remnants of the North Korean People's Army (NKPA). The instrument of destruction was to be the Eighth Army, composed largely of American and South Korean troops and commanded by Lieutenant General Walton Walker. To the east, elements of Major General Edward Almond's X Corps had already reached the Yalu at several spots, and in a few days they would turn west to assist the Eighth Army's offensive. With any luck, the war could end before Christmas.

This final offensive promised to cap not just a brilliant campaign but a stellar career. MacArthur had fought in both world wars, winning the Medal of Honor in each. His operations against the Japanese in World War II were text-book examples of hard-hitting maneuvers. MacArthur's military talent seemed undiminished in Korea.

The North Korean invasion in June 1950 had almost driven the southern forces and their American allies off the peninsula, but MacArthur had dramatically reversed the course of the war with an amphibious assault on the NKPA's flank at Inchon. Within a few weeks, the NKPA was in headlong retreat. MacArthur's troops doggedly pursued the disintegrating enemy northward,

Above: The rugged mountains of North Korea canalized the U.N. troops' advance to the Yalu River and allowed for a devastating Chinese counterstroke.

capturing the North Korean capital of P'yongyang in October before pausing to gather their strength for the final lunge to the Yalu.

The Red Chinese, to be sure, had protested vigorously the U.N. advance toward their border and had on more than one occasion threatened intervention, but MacArthur thought this was just empty posturing. Therefore, in the last half of October he issued orders for a broad-front attack to the Yalu; the Eighth Army and the X Corps would advance independently and as rapidly as possible to bring the war to a speedy conclusion, with the Taebaek Mountains serving as the boundary between the two formations.

At MacArthur's headquarters in Tokyo, optimism ran so high that staff officers were already drawing plans to bring the troops home. This spirit transmitted itself readily to Walker and Almond, who drove their subordinates hard, until the foremost units began to lose touch with one another in the rush to the Yalu.

The Chinese remained the only sour note: the People's Republic of China had begun to ship "volunteers" across the Yalu into North Korea to fight alongside their fraternal socialist comrades-in-arms. Clashes with Chinese units took place in late October and in the first week of November, causing MacArthur's intelligence officers to estimate that parts of twelve Chinese People's Liberation Army (PLA) divisions—perhaps 70,000 soldiers—were in North Korea. The question was, what were China's intentions?

MacArthur discounted the likelihood of an all-out Chinese commitment in support of a North Korea on the verge of defeat, or of the danger to his own forces if they did make this commitment. He held the fighting abilities of the PLA in low esteem, particularly given their lack of modern equipment. He also believed that aerial attacks against the Yalu bridges and Korean road network would slow the flow of Chinese reinforcements to a trickle. Indeed, the Chinese offered no serious resistance to the U.N. advance after November 6, and aerial reconnaissance revealed none of the massing of troops or logistical activity considered necessary for the launching of a major attack. As Thanksgiving Day approached, MacArthur and his principal staff concluded that the Chinese had no stomach for a fight. More important, the possibility of Chinese intervention did not fit with the euphoric mood of headquarters; planning for it meant abandoning hopes for an early end to the war, a feat few—including MacArthur—were psychologically prepared for. As a result, he did not issue any modification to his original orders.

But the conclusion was wishful thinking based on a fundamental error of intelligence analysis. MacArthur and his staff were reckoning in Western terms; they measured the PLA as though it were a modern mechanized army fighting in the American style instead of an army of tough, foot-slogging peasant soldiers employing a tactical style all their own. Hardened by years of guerrilla fighting during the Chinese Civil War, the typical PLA soldier was a master of the art of camouflage, inured to hardship and capable of prodigious feats of marching; he shrugged off aerial attacks as minor annoyances and carried his food and much of his ammunition on his back.

In truth, the PLA had been pouring troops into Korea since mid-October, and these troops had been holing up among the inhospitable peaks of the Taebaeks. By October 25, the Chinese had more than 300,000 men (more than four times MacArthur's latest estimate) waiting to ambush the U.N. army.

That army, meanwhile, was rapidly placing itself in extreme peril. Northern Korea is a jumble of steep mountains and knife-edge ridges, and its few good roads wind through narrow valleys blanketed by snow in mid-November. Divisions were already having trouble maintaining contact with one another across the nightmarish terrain, a task made even more difficult by plunging temperatures and the American soldier's predilection

General Douglas MacArthur, seen here sporting his trademark corncob pipe, dark glasses, and crushed cap, was one of the twentieth century's most brilliant military strategists.

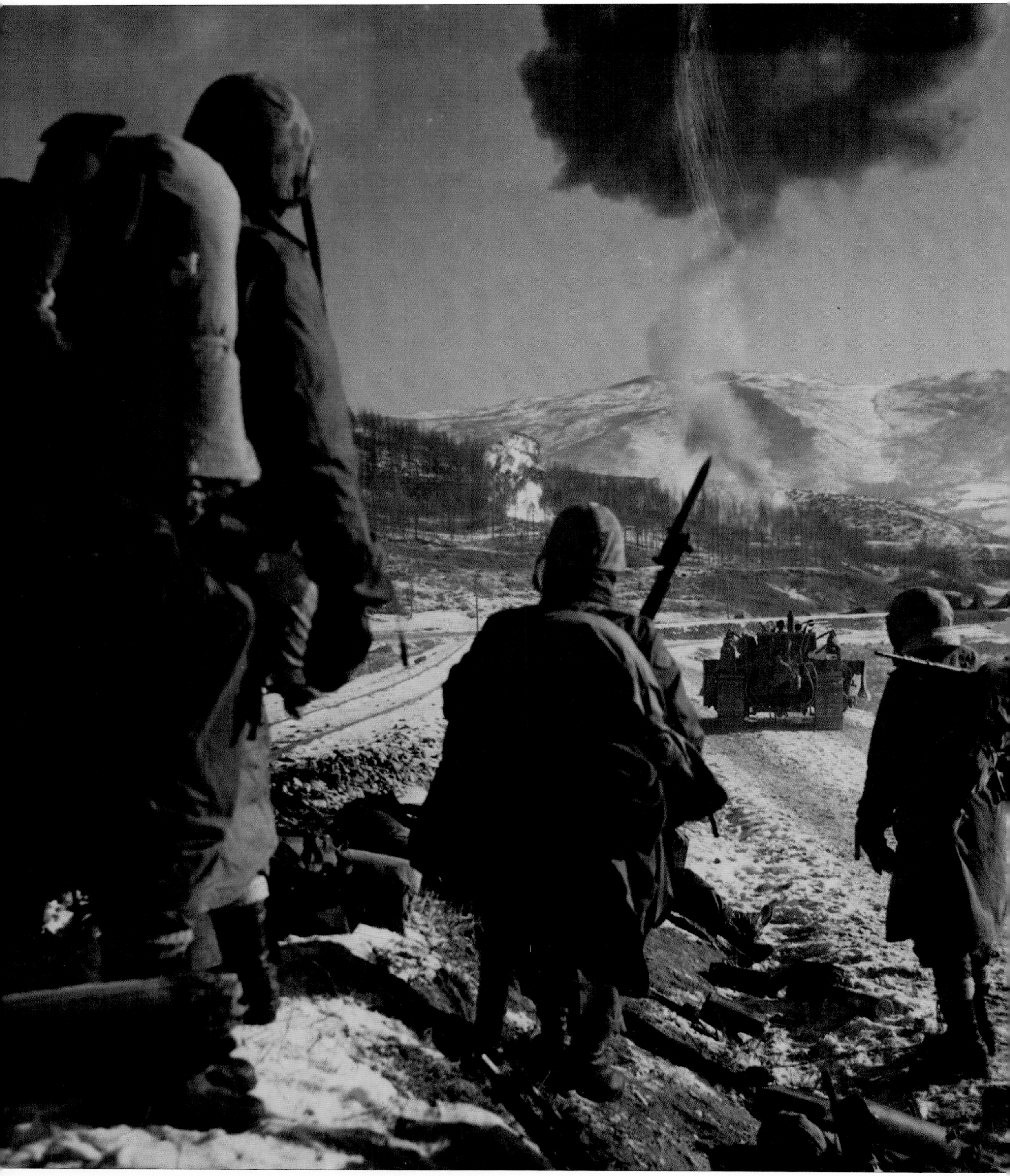

for remaining roadbound. Walker, not as sanguine about the impact of Chinese intervention as were his fellow commanders, pulled back his units somewhat to reestablish contact among his subordinate elements. Almond, on the other hand, concurred wholeheartedly with MacArthur's assessment and actually quickened the pace of his advance. As a result, not only were the X Corps' 100,000 men spread over a chunk of terrain the size of West Virginia, but a widening gap also opened between the Eighth Army and Almond's Corps.

As night fell on October 25, the PLA struck the Eighth Army columns strung out along the snaking tracks that passed for roads in the North Korean mountains near the Ch'ongch'on River. Hordes of Chinese erupted from narrow passes or skidded along treacherous ridgelines to outflank their enemy. In their mustard-yellow quilted jackets, the PLA infantry moved in small groups of forty or fewer to pin down centers of resistance. Rather than moving in the human waves of popular imagination, they favored a creeping approach, using all available cover, to within hand-grenade range; they then used grenades, light mortars, and supporting machine guns to work over the opposition, followed by a short rush to finish the fight. Simultaneously, fast-moving columns worked their way deep into rear areas, ambushing convoys and smashing U.S. fuel depots, motor parks, and ammunition dumps.

By daylight, the eastern flank of the Eighth Army had been pushed back considerably, but neither Walker nor the command at Tokyo was unduly concerned. The Chinese, for the most part, suspended their attacks during the day to avoid American airpower, a sensible precaution that deluded the Americans into thinking that the worst was over. When the attack continued over the nights of November 26 and 27, however, alarm bells began to ring.

Except in Tokyo. There, in the comfort of their offices, intelligence officers were reluctant to admit that they might have misjudged Chinese capabilities and intentions, claiming that it was impossi-ble to tell if this was indeed the launch of a major offensive. As a result, while the Eighth Army was fighting for its life on November 27 in the face of seventeen PLA divisions, no extraordinary warnings were transmitted to the X Corps.

It might have been too late, in any case. Almond's incautious dash to the Yalu had left a gap of 70 miles (112km) between his 1st Marine Division at Chosin Reservoir and the main body of the 7th Infantry Division to the east. The Marines' left flank also hung in thin air as Walker's right continued to give way. Into this vacuum swung seven PLA divisions, entrapping the bulk of the 1st Marines and the 7th Division's 31st Regimental Combat Team (RCT) at Chosin.

Though MacArthur had badly misjudged the extent of the Chinese intervention, he quickly recognized the gravity of the situation. During a hurried conference with Walker and Almond in Tokyo on November 28, he ordered an immediate suspension of the offensive and gave both commanders great latitude in withdrawing their forces southward. Thus began the longest fighting retreat in American history.

The Eighth Army began its trek south on the following day, with the PLA continuously hammering its right, seeking to trap the American forces against the Yellow Sea. Walker abandoned P'yongyang on December 5, leaving the city aflame along with mountains of American supplies. Never able to relieve the pressure on his eastern flank long enough to dig in to solid defensive positions, Walker continued to move his forces back until he was killed in a traffic accident two days before Christmas. General Matthew Ridgway took over the Eighth Army shortly thereafter, but it was not until February 1951 that he finally stabilized the line and halted the Chinese, more than 250 miles (400km) from the Ch'ongch'on.

The X Corps, meanwhile, withdrew with great difficulty to Hungnam and its surrounding ports. At Chosin, the 31st RCT had been effectively destroyed; on December 1, it numbered only 385 able-bodied soldiers out of its original 3,000. These survivors managed to link up with the 1st Marine Division, which then cut its way free to the coast in one of the greatest feats of American arms—though at the cost of an additional 2,600 casualties, including nearly 400 dead. From there, they were evacuated to South Korea, leaving North Korea to the communists once again.

◆ ◆ ◆

A peasant army had outmaneuvered and defeated a modern force that both outnumbered and outgunned it, by taking advantage of American tactical blunders, overconfidence, and inability to fight effectively in rugged terrain. The key strength of the People's Liberation Army lay in its maneuverability—not through motorization or speed but through the exploitation of its superior mobility in mountainous country.

In fact, a common thread running through these defeats is the loser's inability to maneuver—either because he failed to compensate for difficult terrain, as in Korea and around Suomussalmi, or because he deliberately pinned himself down, as Hitler did at Stalingrad. This theme is also reflected in the final case study, where a commander blundered away a dearly bought victory by pausing on the threshold of success. But unlike the other three examples, this deliberate sacrifice of mobility did not arise from overconfidence. Instead, it demonstrated that caution can sometimes be as deadly a sin.

Opposite: U.S. Marines operating in the hills of Korea while Marine air support pounds Chinese army positions in the background.

Golan Heights

They had a great many tanks, but they didn't know how to fight.

—Israeli tanker

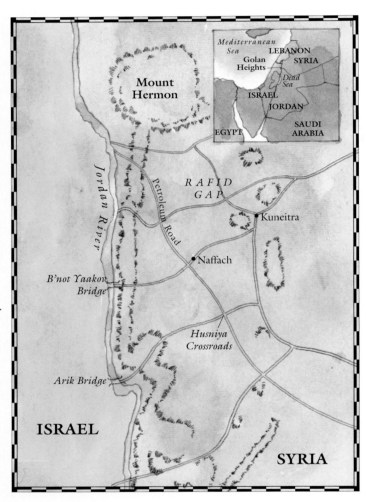

Above: The Golan Heights formed a narrow rampart overlooking the Jordan River, Israel's border with its hostile neighbor Syria.

It was October 6, 1973, the first day of the Yom Kippur War, and the Syrian surprise assault to seize the Golan Heights was not going well. Occupied by the Israelis since 1967, the Golan was the rough edge of an escarpment that ended precipitously along the east bank of the Jordan River. Possession of the Heights conferred a significant military advantage upon the owner: for the Israelis, controlling this position prevented the Syrians from attacking the lush farmland of the Huleh Valley, the centerpiece of Israeli agriculture. For the Syrians, it was an ideal spot from which to bombard Israeli agricultural settlements.

To take the Golan, the Syrians had rebuilt an army that had been destroyed in the Six Day War of 1967. Five divisions and several independent brigades mustering 1,200 tanks and 600 heavy artillery pieces formed up in two echelons along a front that was less than 50 miles (80km) wide. Facing them were sixty Israeli tanks and a handful of infantry battalions manning bunkers along the cease-fire line that had been established in 1967.

The Syrian General Staff had few illusions about the cost of overcoming this paltry opposition. They knew better than anyone about the extremely high quality of the Israeli Defense Force (IDF) but believed that their own numerical superiority would more than compensate for any deficiencies in their training or officer corps. The attack, timed to coincide with an Egyptian crossing of the Suez Canal, would lead off with three divisions advancing abreast in the wake of massive artillery barrages, with two armored divisions poised two hours behind to exploit any breakthroughs. Simultaneously, heliborne commandos would capture the bridges on the Jordan River, sealing off the Golan from Israeli reinforcements. Within thirty hours, the Heights would be Syrian.

But from the beginning, the Syrians were victims of their own caution. President Assad, the dictatorial ruler of Syria, withdrew his finest, and most politically reliable, division from the order of battle, intent upon preserving it as a prop for his regime, should the war go badly. The deep commando strikes were also canceled for fear of wrecking this elite branch of the Syrian armed forces, a move that allowed the Israelis to reinforce the Golan throughout the crucial first days of the attack.

The assault itself also misfired. The two best approaches to the Jordan—the Kuneitra Gap in the north and the Rafid Gap in the south—were allotted a division each, with the 9th Syrian Infantry Division consigned to a supporting role in the rougher terrain of the center. But even the two gaps presented the attacker with serious obstacles to maneuver, canalizing the assaulting tanks and infantry into narrow passes and shallow, rock-strewn valleys reinforced by antitank ditches and minefields. The Israeli defenders overcame their initial surprise and used the natural cover brilliantly, surrendering ground only grudgingly as the northern and southern gaps became choked with the flaming hulks of Syrian armored vehicles.

But neither the IDF nor the Syrian General Staff counted on the drive by the 9th Division's commander, Colonel Hassan Tourkmani. Fully cognizant of

Desert Storm

The most one-sided defeat in modern military history, a campaign that will be studied in war colleges and military academies for centuries to come, was the rout of the Iraqi army in Kuwait. The fourth largest army in the world was mauled during 100 hours of fighting. But it needn't have turned out that way.

When Saddam Hussein invaded tiny Kuwait in August 1990, he provoked the United States into heading an allied coalition that was determined to eject him from the oil-rich kingdom—by force if necessary. But deploying and readying such a force would take months, despite ready access to excellent airfields and port facilities in Saudi Arabia.

Hussein could easily have precluded the buildup with an immediate invasion of northeastern Saudi Arabia. The only elements opposing him throughout August and into September were ineffectual Saudi National Guard units, a few battalions of attack helicopters, and the American 82nd Airborne Division. While the 82nd was well trained,

it was too lightly equipped to stop an Iraqi thrust across the open desert (in fact, the paratroopers jokingly referred to themselves as speed bumps in the sand). Once in possession of the Saudi Persian Gulf ports, Hussein could have forced the allies to make concessions or undertake a costly amphibious assault to liberate the occupied territories. In either case, the ultimate outcome would have been less humiliating.

his own troops' tactical shortcomings, he ruthlessly exploited the stoic courage of the Syrian soldiers. Tourkmani, initially held up along the cease-fire line, ordered his lead tank battalion to clear a lane through the Israeli minefields by simply driving straight ahead. Tank after tank slewed aside after striking a mine or brewed up under the fire of the Israeli defenders, only to be pushed out of the way by the vehicle that followed. It cost him a battalion, but the minefield was breached by nightfall, and Tourkmani led the rest of his division through the opening and into the heart of the Golan Heights.

Bypassing Israeli border fortifications, the Syrian 51st Independent Tank Brigade—Tourkmani's spearhead—roared into the night. By 10 P.M., it had reached the critical Hushniya crossroads and swung northward along the Petro-

leum Road. Tourkmani planned to outflank the Israelis who were blocking the Kuneitra Gap, but his attack lost its impetus in the dark defiles of the Golan, which was expertly defended by a few Israeli tanks. Nevertheless, the Syrian leader continued to press his men forward at great cost, whittling away at the IDF units that were holding him back. Two hours after midnight, only a single Israeli tank still clung desperately to its position along the Petroleum Road.

Now was the time for a bold commitment of the Syrian second echelon. The 9th Division had punched through farther and faster than expected, but it had reached the end of its tether. Tourkmani had only enough strength to protect his own flanks and maintain pressure on the weakening Israelis, who were struggling to contain him. Major General Yousef Chakour, Chief of the Syrian

General Staff, knew of Tourkmani's success at Hushniya but hesitated to order the reserve forward. He had not anticipated a breakthrough in the center and still harbored hopes of penetrating the Rafid or Kuneitra Gaps—and thus he waffled. Five critical hours passed before he finally directed the 1st Tank Division toward Husniya. The division required another six hours to reach the crossroads and move into the attack.

It was time enough for the desperate IDF. Damaged tanks were hastily repaired, manned with scratch crews, and sent forward; arriving reservists, who had been at home a few hours earlier, observing the Jewish holy day of Yom Kippur, were dispatched in small groups to the front, where brigade and battalion commanders directed them to wherever the danger was greatest. By 9 A.M. on October 7, the IDF had mustered a

The poorly trained and poorly led Syrian soldiers at Golan Heights lacked initiative and tactical finesse, but their courage never flagged.

dozen operable tanks on either side of the Petroleum Road, with several more platoons on the way.

This scratch force could not stop the 1st Division attack that developed around 11 A.M., but their doomed struggle cost the Syrians the one thing that they could not afford: time. A swirling mechanized battle revolved around the Israeli base at Naffach; outnumbered ten to one, IDF platoons fought Syrian battalions, yielding ground only when threatened with encirclement. As daylight began to fail, the Syrians finally shook free of the tenacious Israelis around Naffach and headed for the B'not Yaakov bridge over the Jordan. They arrived within four miles (6.4km)

Israeli tankers, most of them reservists, held the line against overwhelming odds. These jubilant soldiers, on the road to Damascus, celebrate victory in the Golan.

of this strategic crossing by nightfall. Unwilling to continue the advance in the darkness, the 1st Division halted, planning on a renewed attack at first light.

But this proved to be the high-water mark of the Syrian assault on the Golan. Sufficient Israeli reinforcements were now flowing into the region to stem the Syrian tide and ultimately inflict a stinging defeat. The Arabs were sent reeling back toward their capital; a cease-fire ended the war on October 23.

✦ ✦ ✦

Had General Chakour committed his reserves within an hour or two of the news of Tourkmani's breakthrough, the 1st Armored could have driven to the Jordan virtually unopposed, regaining their freedom to maneuver. Had he made his decision even an hour earlier than he did, the scales might have tipped in favor of the Syrians. But by hesitating to modify his plan and succumbing to the temptation of waiting to clarify the situation, Chakour frittered away the chance for victory, purchased at the cost of much blood from his stout-hearted soldiers. Such slim margins separate triumph from defeat in modern armored warfare.

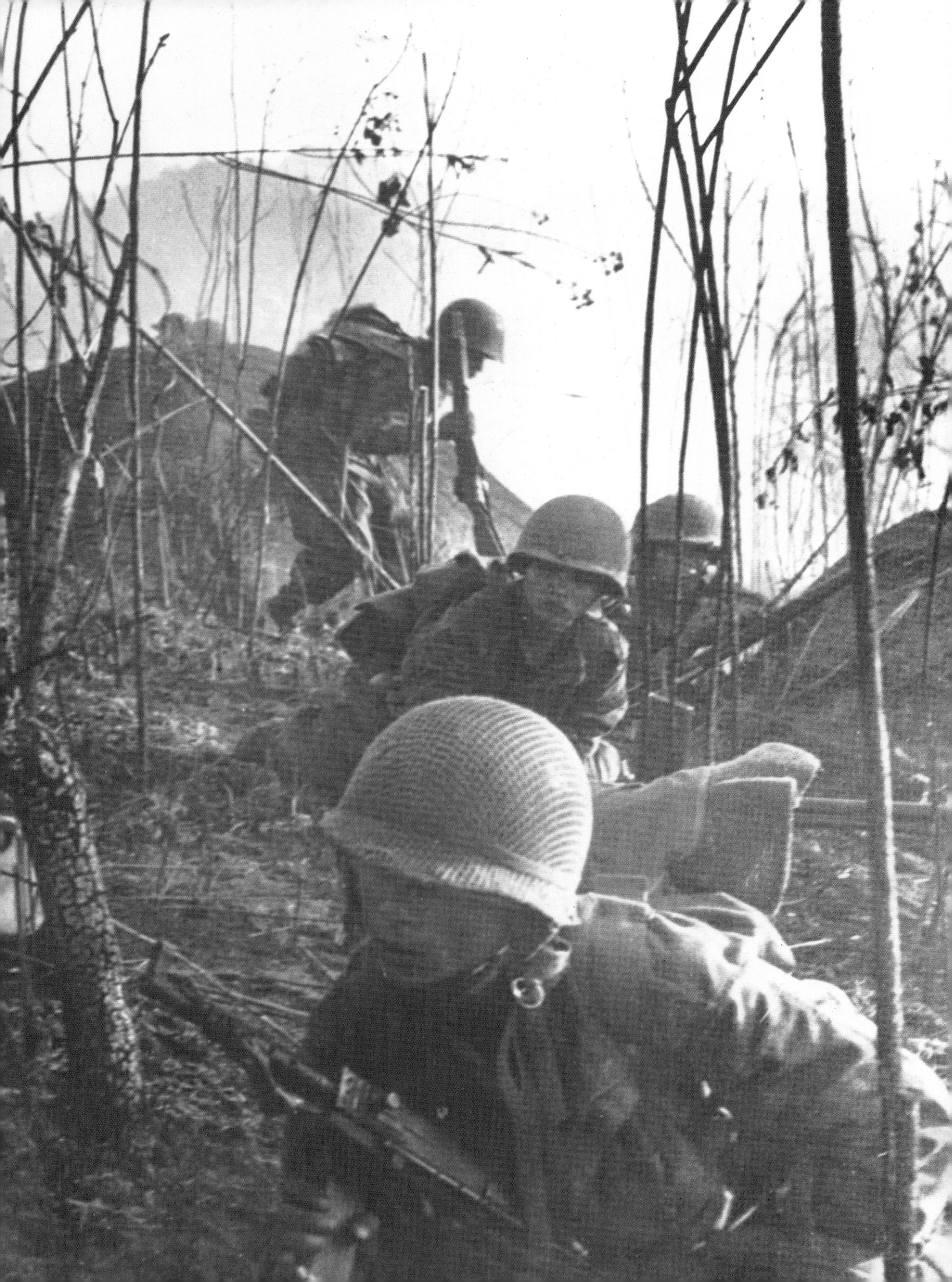

2

ANUAL • DIEN BIEN PHU

TET OFFENSIVE • PANJSHIR VALLEY

Guerrilla Warfare

Guerrilla war occurs whenever one side is too weak to face the enemy in a stand-up fight but too stubborn to lay down its arms. Because he cannot hope to defeat his opponent in a single campaign, the guerrilla resorts to a protracted form of warfare; his primary tools are the hit-and-run raid, the ambush, and the surprise attack. He seeks refuge in terrain in which conventional armies have difficulty operating or submerges himself among the populace. He relies on secrecy, speed, and dispersion to elude the enemy, wearing down his opponent while building his own strength. His hope is to drain the enemy's will and resources through attrition as his own grow, until the day comes when the balance of power tilts in his favor.

Those who oppose him possess far greater striking power, but they face a dilemma: the guerrilla must be denied access to food, money, and manpower, but this can be done only by securing the countryside or long stretches of border. If this is attempted, the conventional army faces defeat in detail by a guerrilla force that, while weaker overall, is free to concentrate at any point for battle. Alternately, if an army is massed for a decisive blow, the nimbler guerrilla

can easily avoid it, and thus the countryside is left unguarded.

The key to winning the guerrilla war, then, is balance. A conventional army must disperse to counter the guerrilla forces without exposing itself to defeat. The guerrilla must weigh the short-term benefits of each battle with the long-term imperative of simply surviving to fight another day. Failure to follow these simple rules has led to several of the more spectacular military disasters of the twentieth century.

Guerrilla warfare is as old as war itself, but it became popular again in the last hundred years as a way for colonial peoples to eject their European colonizers. The colonial empires began to totter in the years between the world wars, but it wasn't until after World War II that the empires came apart. Fired by ideology, religion, or nationalism (and in some cases by all three), native peoples from Africa and Asia began fighting for independence. Too weak to sweep out the Europeans in most cases, many of these rebels resorted to guerrilla warfare. For some, such as the Berber tribes of North Africa, guerrilla war came naturally, an extension of their traditional style of warfare.

French Vietnamese paratroopers on patrol near Dien Bien Phu.

35

Anual

I became tired of cutting throats.

—Rif warrior

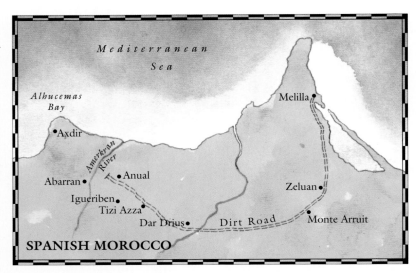

During the early part of the twentieth century, the mountains of northern Morocco harbored a fiercely independent group of tribes, a collective of part native Berber stock, part descendants of Arab invaders. Known as the Rif, these tribes had maintained control of their mountain fastnesses for a thousand years, and successive rulers of Morocco had learned the cost of trying to subdue the Rif warriors. In 1921, Spanish invaders tangled with the Rif, much to their sorrow—they suffered the worst defeat of a European army in African history.

Spain had occupied enclaves on the North African seacoast since the sixteenth century, but had rarely penetrated farther inland. In 1904, stung by their recent loss of Caribbean colonies and the Philippines during the Spanish-American War, Spain resolved to carve a new empire from northern Morocco, situated just across the Strait of Gibraltar. For nearly two decades afterward, the Spanish clashed with native tribesmen, seeking to establish control over what had become Spanish Morocco. In 1920, they began yet another campaign. One force operated with some success in the western part of the colony, while a second force of 20,000 Spanish soldiers and 4,000 native auxiliaries prepared to campaign against the eastern tribes, using the port of Melilla as its base. This army, under the command of General Manuel Silvestre, aimed to pacify the Rif tribes and establish control over Alhucemas Bay, con-

Top: The imperialist ambitions of King Alphonso XIII of Spain doomed thousands of his soldiers. Above: The Spanish attempt to expand their coastal enclave around Melilla to encompass Alhucemas Bay met disaster near Anual.

sidered a perfect harbor for future campaigns against the continent's interior.

Silvestre—an often-wounded veteran of numerous campaigns and the court favorite of King Alphonso XIII, renowned as much for his sexual prowess as for his martial ardor—regarded the success of the western campaign with envy. Determined to outdo the other commanders in Spanish Morocco, he departed Melilla and pushed into the surrounding mountains. As the Spanish moved forward, they established a series of forts and blockhouses to guard their line of communications. Some, such as the posts at Anual and Monte Arruit, were fairly elaborate, with garrisons of 800 or more, but the greater number were scarcely larger than small houses, housing perhaps a

dozen soldiers each. By May 1921, the Spaniards had occupied over 2,500 square miles (6,500 sq km) of territory, against negligible resistance. Silvestre felt confident enough to attempt a crossing of the swift-flowing Amerkran River, the last major obstacle between his army and the Bay of Alhucemas. Despite the warnings of several native advisers that such a move would trigger Rif attacks, a detachment forded the river in late May and established a camp near Abarran.

Unfortunately for the Spanish, Silvestre's confidence was misplaced. The Spanish army in Morocco was an exceedingly poor tool for empire building. The largely untrained conscripts, shoddily clothed and paid less than native laborers, suffered in filthy billets and hospitals, subsisting on insufficient rations. The Spanish officer corps was, for the most part, execrable. Many supported themselves on the black market by selling supplies meant for their men, and few troubled themselves to train or even visit their own units. Moreover, the brash general disdained the fighting abilities of the "Moors," as he sneeringly termed them. Consequently, Silvestre had scattered his demoralized troops in 144 separate outposts, many without communications, extra ammunition, or easy access to water.

Opposing Silvestre's men were forces led by Si Mohammed ben Abd-el-Krim, a former judge in the Spanish colonial administration, a linguist, newspaper

The Bay of Alhucemas on the northern coast of Morocco was the object of General Manuel Silvestre's ill-fated expedition.

editor, religious and legal scholar—and chieftain of the Beni Uriaghel, the most belligerent of the Rif tribes. Unprepossessing in appearance, portly, and balding, Abd-el-Krim limped because of an injury suffered while escaping a Spanish prison, and he nursed an implacable hatred for his former employers. He led only 3,000 fighters, but they were formidable warriors, fired with religious enthusiasm and the promise of plunder. Provoked by the renewed Spanish advance, Abd-el-Krim struck in the last days of May.

On June 1, native troops in Abarran mutinied. In conjunction with Rif attacks, they overwhelmed the Spanish garrison, killing 179 out of 250 men there. Silvestre, dallying in Melilla, considered the affair an isolated incident and did nothing to strengthen his position in the mountains. Nevertheless, the massacre caused considerable unease among the isolated garrisons, and the Spanish high commissioner ordered Silvestre to refrain from further action.

But the headstrong general refused to be leashed. After some weeks of rela-

tive quiet, Silvestre ordered a new camp constructed at Igueriben, three miles (4.8km) south of Anual. On July 18, Abd-el-Krim launched an assault against the partly completed post. For several days, the garrison resisted stoutly—one of the few bright spots for Spanish arms—but the camp had no water supply, and the men were soon reduced to drinking their own urine for survival. Repeated Spanish efforts to break through the ring of Rif warriors were rebuked by tribesmen who employed captured machine guns in the narrow gorges. Finally, a few weary survivors escaped to Anual, the rest of the garrison having been massacred by gleeful Beni Uriaghel.

Silvestre had reached Anual with about 5,000 soldiers, just in time to find himself surrounded by fresh Rif forces advancing from Igueriben. The fort at Anual, dominated on all sides by mountains swarming with hostile warriors, was clearly untenable, but retreat also seemed impossible. Silvestre, recognizing now that his own arrogance had placed his army in a hopeless position,

seems to have suffered a mental breakdown: he directed his officers to prepare for withdrawal on July 22 but offered them no detailed orders. The retreat began under the noses of the alert Rif tribesmen, who attacked the frightened Spanish columns, which soon dissolved in panic. General Silvestre was last seen frantically urging his troops to "run, run, the bogeyman is coming!"

The Spanish troops needed little encouragement. They stampeded eastward, throwing down their weapons and abandoning their wagons and artillery in headlong flight. Silvestre did not emerge from Anual, though reports differ as to whether he died in battle or by his own hand. His deputy, one General Navarro, struggled valiantly to hold together a rear guard, but his tiny band of stalwarts was overwhelmed by Spanish fugitives, the Rif hard on their heels. One by one, each of the tiny blockhouses between Anual and Monte Arruit fell into the hands of the Rif.

As news of the disaster spread, individual Spanish garrisons abandoned their posts without orders, trying to make their way to the coast. Mean-while, the other Rif tribes, eager to join the fray now that victory was assured, fell upon these isolated platoons and companies as they hurried through the mountain passes and slaughtered the Spanish soldiers without mercy, adding to the general panic. Navarro and a few thousand stunned survivors stumbled into Monte Arruit, where the plucky Spaniard tried to make a stand, unwilling to abandon his wounded men to the Rif. However, there was little food and no medical supplies at the fort; more important, the outpost was nearly a mile (1.6km) from the nearest source of water. After waiting in vain for relief from Melilla, Navarro finally surrendered to the Rif, who promptly killed every Spaniard in the fort save the commander and a few others.

The scope of the disaster was unprecedented: Spanish rule in the eastern part of the colony was reduced to the port of Melilla; 5,000 square miles (13,000 sq km) of territory had been reclaimed by the Rif; nearly 18,000 Spanish soldiers (90 percent of the original force) had been slain, for the Berbers took few prisoners; and mountains of equipment, supplies, and weapons were lost to the tribesmen. Moreover, all of this had been accomplished by a Rif army that had never numbered more than 4,000 warriors.

Silvestre committed one of the classic blunders of guerrilla war: in an effort to control territory, he dispersed his inept units too widely, exposing them to defeat in detail by a smaller force. Thirty years later, on the other side of the world, French General Henri Navarre would try the opposite tack: striving to suppress the Viet Minh in Indochina, Navarre concentrated a magnificent but outnumbered fighting force in a single location in order to lure the elusive enemy to battle. Unfortunately for himself, his army, and the French colonial empire, he got exactly what he wanted.

Above: A Moroccan sniper hiding out in the craggy hills of his homeland.

Dien Bien Phu

We're blowing up everything. Adieu.

—Last radio message from Dien Bien Phu

On March 15, 1954, Colonel Charles Piroth retreated alone to his bunker in the beleaguered fortress of Dien Bien Phu. The usually jovial commander of artillery had just witnessed the destruction of most of his guns by communist artillery that ringed the post. Three months earlier, Piroth had boasted that his cannoneers would smash any enemy guns brought to bear against Dien Bien Phu; instead, it was the Viet Minh gunners who were systematically pounding the garrison into dust. Piroth knew that the garrison could not survive without artillery, and he had no desire to witness its inevitable defeat. Piroth, having lost an arm in Italy during World War II, could not cock his pistol by himself, so he picked up a grenade. Lying down on his cot, he pulled the pin with his teeth and held the grenade to his chest. The explosion went unnoticed amid the din of battle.

The French fortress at Dien Bien Phu had been established in November 1953 to control the only road between central Laos and northern Vietnam. General Henri Navarre, commander of the French Expeditionary Corps in Indochina, initially hoped to use the airfield there as a supply base for patrols against the Viet Minh insurgents and to block communist access to the rich rice harvest in Laos. Consequently, French engineers hastily constructed a series of strongpoints around the air base, and

Top: General Giap, the guiding genius of North Vietnam's thirty-year war against the French and the Americans. Above: France's "fortress" at Dien Bien Phu was overextended, overly reliant on aerial resupply, and dominated by the surrounding jungled hills.

planes brought in a 6,000-man garrison, complete with artillery and tanks.

By February 1954, it was clear that Navarre's original plan had failed. The Viet Minh had quickly sealed off the fortress, preventing the French from interfering with the flow of troops or rice between Laos and Vietnam. Moreover,

intelligence reports indicated that communist reinforcements were converging on Dien Bien Phu; especially disturbing was the apparent concentration of ammunition and heavy-caliber artillery.

Navarre would have been well advised at this point to evacuate the garrison; it could serve little purpose in Dien Bien Phu, and the manpower was desperately needed elsewhere. Instead, Navarre opted to reinforce Dien Bien Phu with some of his finest units, including elite paratroopers, elements of the Foreign Legion, and colonial units from French North Africa—using them as the bait in a new strategy that he hoped would win the war for control of Indochina.

For seven years, the French had been fighting a losing battle against Vietnamese nationalists and communists to retain their colony. The Viet Minh, trained in guerrilla warfare against Japanese invaders during World War II, had turned on their former colonial masters when the French returned in 1946. Led by the legendary General Vo Nguyen Giap, the Viet Minh had control over most of northern Vietnam by 1953, reducing French occupation to an enclave around Hanoi. Giap, employing a mixture of irregular and more conventional warriors, had constructed a force of six "regular" divisions to supplement his guerrillas. Navarre, the latest in a succession of French commanders, believed that de-

Viet Minh regulars on patrol in a communist-controlled city in Indochina.

stroying the core of regular divisions would allow the French the maneuvering freedom that they needed to regain control of the countryside.

Navarre hoped to draw Giap into an assault on Dien Bien Phu and administer the Viet Minh a decisive defeat. His subordinates argued against the strategy, pointing out that the fortress lay in a basin surrounded by high ground and would consequently be difficult to defend. Moreover, Dien Bien Phu was cut off from the rest of the French army by miles of largely trackless jungle. Navarre arrogantly dismissed the warnings. The communists could not actually take the out-

post, he reasoned, because of three factors: first, they could not bring to bear sufficient heavy artillery in the hilly jungle ringing Dien Bien Phu, nor could they amass sufficient supplies to support more than a single assault division. Second, French bombers and artillery would smash any attack that might threaten the garrison. And third, the garrison could be supplied by air with sufficient fuel, food, and ammunition to prolong resistance indefinitely.

Unfortunately, Navarre was wrong on all counts. Coolie labor hacked trails through the jungle, lugged disassembled artillery into positions overlooking the French defensive works, and stockpiled enough supplies to sustain not one but four full divisions for the attack. By early March, 37,000 Viet Minh troops backed by 200 heavy-artillery pieces prepared to descend on the reinforced garrison defending Dien Bien Phu, which consisted of a mere 11,000

French, Vietnamese, foreign legionnaires, and North Africans.

When the attack began on March 13, the weakness of the French position became immediately apparent. The communist-held hills dominated the entire outpost in the valley below. In their jungle-clad firing positions, enemy gunners could fire on every square foot of the fortress—including the vital airstrip—while remaining virtually invulnerable to air attack or counterbattery fire. Outlying French strong points were poorly sited, difficult to resupply, and too far from the main camp. Most succumbed quickly.

By the time that Piroth killed himself—only two days into the attack—the handwriting was already on the wall. Within a week, the garrison commander had withdrawn into his own command bunker, where he remained for the duration, virtually abandoning any active role in the fighting. Meanwhile, his

"I don't want any damn Dinbinfoo!"

In 1967, U.S. Army general William Westmoreland decided that the best way to lure the Viet Cong into a decisive battle was to thrust a small American force deep into the jungled hills near the Laotian border. The outpost, near the small town of Khe Sanh, would serve as the bait to draw the communists into a trap where they could be decimated by American firepower. If that sounds familiar, it should. Many observers, including President Lyndon Johnson (whose pithy comment is recorded above), cautioned Westmoreland that he was risking a second Dien Bien Phu. Vietnam's General Giap also regarded Khe Sanh with a sense of déjà vu and soon concentrated four North Vietnamese Army (NVA) divisions in the area, including one that had fought at Dien Bien Phu, along with two regiments of artillery—perhaps some 40,000 men in all.

Khe Sanh certainly looked like Dien Bien Phu. Surrounded by hills, the outpost depended on aerial resupply, as the roads had been cut. The American command post was even located in an old French bunker. But, unnoticed by Giap, there were significant differences this time

around that resulted in a severe drubbing for the NVA. The marines defending Khe Sanh fortified the hilltops that ringed the base, denying the communists their use. Helicopters, which had been unavailable to the French years earlier at Dien Bien Phu, provided a safer and more reliable means of transporting supplies, even when the airstrip was under shellfire. Finally, the Americans were able to call upon much greater air support, including B-52s carrying the world's largest conventional bombs. Giap opened the siege of Khe Sanh on January 20, 1968, and maintained it until early March, but the Vietnamese never came close to seizing the base. Each time his forces concentrated for a strike, they were pounded by artillery and air attack, and the surviving forces were repelled by well-fed, well-armed marines. There were a few worrisome moments, but in the end Giap's divisions limped away from Khe Sanh. Casualty numbers are impossible to pin down with any accuracy, but the NVA certainly lost more than a 1,000 soldiers, all because of Giap's failed attempt to re-create history.

French general Henri Navarre (left), architect of the disastrous strategy of "luring" the Viet Minh to Dien Bien Phu, talking to Bao Dai, the French-controlled puppet ruler of Indochina.

range of Dien Bien Phu's command bunker, the French surrendered.

Navarre had committed 15,000 soldiers to the defense of Dien Bien Phu, including more than 4,000 who had been flown or parachuted in after the siege began. Of these, some 6,000 were killed or listed as missing in action. The remainder, more than half of them wounded, passed into Viet Minh prison camps. Fewer than eighty managed to escape to friendly lines. While the Viet Minh suffered considerably more casualties, including 8,000 dead, the blow to French morale outweighed purely material concerns. Navarre had gotten the stand-up fight he so ardently desired, but the communist insurgents had beaten the French at their own game. As a direct result, French politicians gave up hope of reasserting control over Indochina. In July 1954, they signed an agreement with the Viet Minh to withdraw from the region.

◆ ◆ ◆

The French withdrawal did not bring peace to the region, however. The United States, concerned that a Viet Minh victory in Indochina could spark the further spread of communism in southeast Asia, stepped in to support an anticommunist government in the south. For nearly a decade, American involvement was limited to advisory teams and small special forces units, but in the mid-1960s President Lyndon Johnson authorized the introduction of ground combat troops to Vietnam, greatly expanding the American presence. By 1968, almost half a million American soldiers were defending South Vietnam from communist insurgents (now called the Viet Cong) backed by regular units of the North Vietnamese army. As the Vietnamese New Year approached, both sides were confident that victory was at hand. Both sides were greatly mistaken.

chief of staff suffered a nervous breakdown and had to be flown out. By March 27, enemy shellfire and antiaircraft batteries rendered the airstrip unusable, precluding the evacuation of any additional wounded and reducing the flow of supplies to what could be retrieved from drop zones often swept by enemy fire. The weather also turned bad, further limiting the effectiveness of the French air force in providing close air support for the defenders.

Remarkably, given its handicaps, the garrison held on for nearly two months, surviving incessant barrages and fanatic assaults by wave after wave of crack Viet Minh troops. The prolonged resistance was a testament to the heroism and competence of the outnumbered French and colonial units defending Dien Bien Phu, but tactical prowess could not reverse the blunders of the French high command any more than it could turn back the steady advance of the Viet Minh. On May 7, with the communists within hand-grenade

Tet Offensive

What the hell is going on? I thought we were winning the war!

—Walter Cronkite, on receiving the first
wire reports of the Tet Offensive

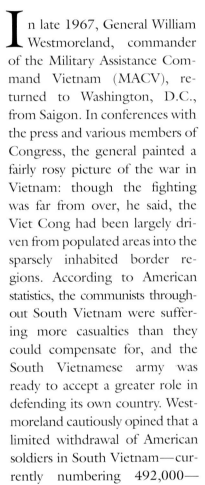

Top: President Lyndon B. Johnson's chance at a second term in office was lost after the disastrous Tet Offensive. Above: The Viet Cong, supposedly on the ropes by early 1968, struck hard all over Vietnam during the Tet Offensive.

In late 1967, General William Westmoreland, commander of the Military Assistance Command Vietnam (MACV), returned to Washington, D.C., from Saigon. In conferences with the press and various members of Congress, the general painted a fairly rosy picture of the war in Vietnam: though the fighting was far from over, he said, the Viet Cong had been largely driven from populated areas into the sparsely inhabited border regions. According to American statistics, the communists throughout South Vietnam were suffering more casualties than they could compensate for, and the South Vietnamese army was ready to accept a greater role in defending its own country. Westmoreland cautiously opined that a limited withdrawal of American soldiers in South Vietnam—currently numbering 492,000—might "be undertaken beginning late in 1968." The straight-backed, silver-haired old warrior, tanned, fit, and bedecked with ribbons reflecting a lifetime of military service, exuded confidence and heartened many in the United States who had begun to harbor doubts over the wisdom of U.S. involvement.

In North Vietnam, a skinny and stooped old man wearing a rumpled uniform began to prepare for a general offensive that he did not believe in. General Vo Nguyen Giap, victor of Dien Bien Phu and now minister of defense in North Vietnam, had argued against a massive attack in the south but

had been overruled by his government. Despite his own reservations, he would not hold back. Tens of thousands of North Vietnamese regulars had infiltrated South Vietnam to bolster local units of the Viet Cong. Other units of the NVA were concentrated along the sinuous South Vietnamese border, where

they had drawn many American combat units away from southern towns and villages. Throughout the south—in caves and labyrinthine tunnel systems, in swamps and forests, and sometimes in urban hideaways—legions of intensively trained commandos, known to the communists as *dac cong*, prepared to spearhead the assault.

The plan for the general offensive was simple. On Tet, the Lunar New Year, thousands of South Vietnamese soldiers would be home on leave during the traditional holiday truce. Few American or southern units would maintain a high state of security. Taking advantage of their enemies' lowered guard, the Viet Cong would launch simultaneous attacks across the country, aiming to paralyze military headquarters, seize control of the larger urban centers, and spark a popular uprising. NVA main-force units would back up Viet Cong successes and brush aside the south's Army of the Republic of Vietnam (ARVN), which Giap contemptuously believed to be a paper tiger. Giap had no illusions about defeating the Americans outright, but he believed that with the ARVN destroyed and the south overrun, the prospect of digging out the communists might wilt American resolve.

Contrary to popular belief, the Tet Offensive was not a surprise to MACV. Preparations for such a massive offensive could not be completely disguised, and

The Lost Order

There are many tales of armies or intelligence agents—by some stroke of luck or skullduggery—obtaining a copy of their enemy's orders and thereby gaining a considerable advantage in battle. Few of these incidents are as strange, however, as the capture of orders for the Tet Offensive weeks before the massive campaign took place. In the aftermath of a sharp firefight with a band of Viet Cong guerrillas in Vietnam's central highlands, a platoon of the 4th Infantry Division searched the bodies of the enemy dead. Discovered on the body of one communist lieutenant was a copy of the regional command's local directive for Tet, including fairly detailed references to the overall plan. Intelligence officers, recognizing the document's importance, rushed it up the chain of command. Shortly before the offensive, army spokesmen produced the order at the Five O'Clock Follies, the daily press briefings in Saigon as nicknamed by the newsmen. Amazingly, though trumpeted to the media as a triumph of American intelligence, the document seems to have been largely ignored by the MACV, which apparently thought it was a plant of some sort. Certainly, possession of the enemy's game plan does not seem to have benefited the soldiers, sailors, and airmen jolted awake by the early morning Tet assault.

Westmoreland's intelligence officers warned him in December 1967 that some sort of communist operation was brewing. What did catch the Americans off guard was the attack's timing and scale.

The offensive began badly, with an incredible blunder. After six months of meticulous planning for a simultaneous attack across the width and breadth of South Vietnam, seven cities—all of them in Viet Cong Military Region 5—were attacked a day early. None of the operations was particularly successful, and most were handily repulsed by local ARVN units. Why the commanders in this particular area assaulted their targets on January 30, 1968, is still unknown, but they nearly ruined the Tet Offensive before it began.

Luckily for Giap, MACV misinterpreted the premature actions. It had been expecting some sort of major communist operation, and now believed that the offensive had fizzled. Orders putting units throughout the south on "maximum alert" did go out, but the general feeling was that intelligence had clearly overestimated the danger posed by the Viet Cong. Westmoreland and his subordinate commanders went to bed that night confident of their ability to handle any subsequent attacks.

They were rudely awakened at 3 A.M. on January 31. Rocket artillery slammed into Saigon as the city was inundated by thirty-five Viet Cong battalions backed

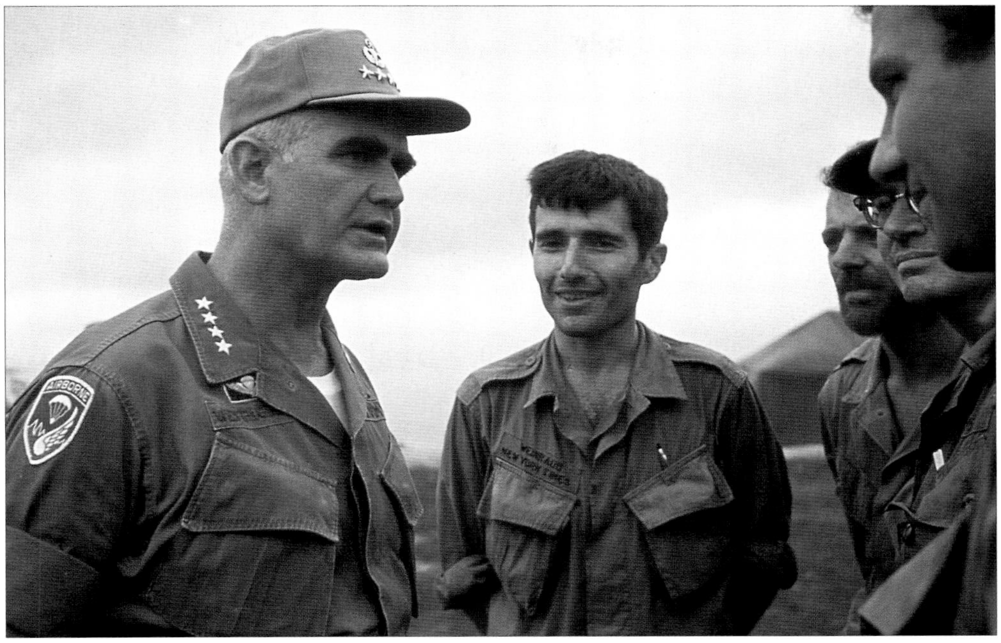

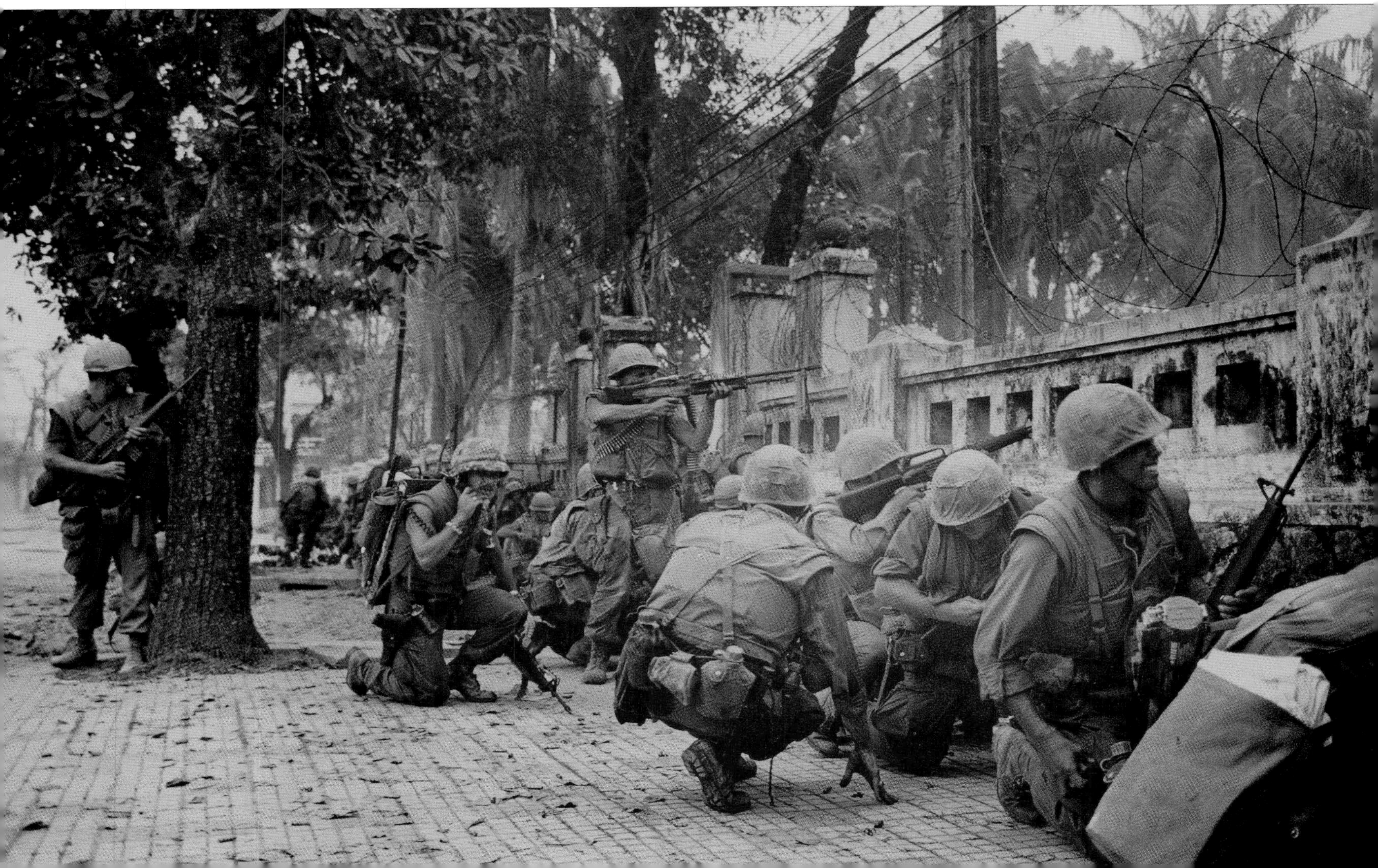

Above: General William Westmoreland speaks to a group of newsmen in the field. The failure of the Tet Offensive destroyed Westmoreland's credibility with the press and the American public. Below: U.S. Marines battle North Vietnamese Army regulars in Hue, the site of one of the war's most vicious pitched battles.

by three NVA divisions. Numerous dac cong detachments blew up mountainous U.S. ammunition dumps, destroyed helicopters and airplanes on the ground, tossed satchel charges into command posts and barracks, and penetrated the U.S. embassy in Saigon. Anti-aircraft guns were towed into position outside major air bases to ambush aircraft as they lifted off; bridges and pipelines throughout the country were sabotaged. More than 100 cities and towns were attacked; aside from Saigon, the Viet Cong seized parts of thirty-nine of South Vietnam's forty-four provincial capitals and seventy-one district capitals. Overall, nearly 70,000 communist troops took part in the Tet Offensive.

Despite the brilliantly coordinated attacks, however, the offensive failed to fulfill the hopes of the North Vietnamese. No uprisings to support the guerrillas took place among the southern populace, and barring some notable exceptions, the ARVN generally gave a good account of itself. After the initial shock wore off, U.S. and South Vietnamese reaction forces quickly cordoned off the occupied cities and began a methodical reduction of the enemy. For once unable to melt into the sheltering countryside, the Viet Cong suffered dreadfully under the hammer of American firepower. By the end of the first week of February, only a thousand or so insurgents remained in Saigon; by mid-month, the communists had been driven out of virtually every urban area that had been seized. In Hue, the ancient seat of the Vietnamese emperors, the fighting was particularly brutal—a grim house-to-house fight against northern regulars —but by February 25, that city had been retaken, signaling an end to the offensive.

Militarily, Tet had been a serious blunder. The communists had displayed a deep misunderstanding of the attitude of the South Vietnamese and the resilience of the ARVN, and consequently exposed their most experienced guerrillas and the elite dac cong to

the unfamiliar territory of urban centers. Trapped in the cities, thousands of irreplaceable guerrilla cadres perished; as an organization, the Viet Cong was destroyed. MACV's estimate of 40,000 enemy casualties is probably greatly exaggerated, but it is indisputable that following Tet, the Viet Cong played no significant role in the war. Moreover, the South Vietnamese government and the ARVN gained greater legitimacy and confidence after turning back the strongest blow yet dealt in the long war—exactly the opposite effect from what the communists had hoped for.

Regardless of its military blunder, the north scored a signal victory in one critical arena. After months of being reassured that the communists were on the ropes, the American public witnessed on their television sets what appeared to be a cunning, strong, and resourceful enemy attacking the heart of South Vietnam. Westmoreland compounded the damage to government credibility when he requested 206,000 additional soldiers in early February. Suddenly, for many Americans, the war seemed a bottomless quagmire. After four years of active involvement, tens of thousands of casualties, and billions of dollars spent, the end was not only no longer in sight, but it seemed to be receding into the distance. Tet proved to be the hinge upon which American public support for the war turned. On March 31, 1968, the Tet Offensive claimed its last victim: Lyndon Johnson, shaken by the offensive and discouraged by the apparent lack of progress in the war, announced in a nationally televised address that he would not seek a second term as president of the United States.

Tet reveals the curious nature of guerrilla war: it is war between two opposing wills as much as between two opposing armies. As such, even military idiocy—and Tet was exactly that—can produce moral victory. Alternately, on a purely military level, Westmoreland's response to the offensive was

Left: The average age of the U.S. soldier in Vietnam was nineteen. This youngster was photographed in 1968, during the peak of U.S. involvement. Above: ARVN soldiers pass two victims of the Tet Offensive. The ARVN performed creditably in the offensive, belying Giap's estimation of its reliability.

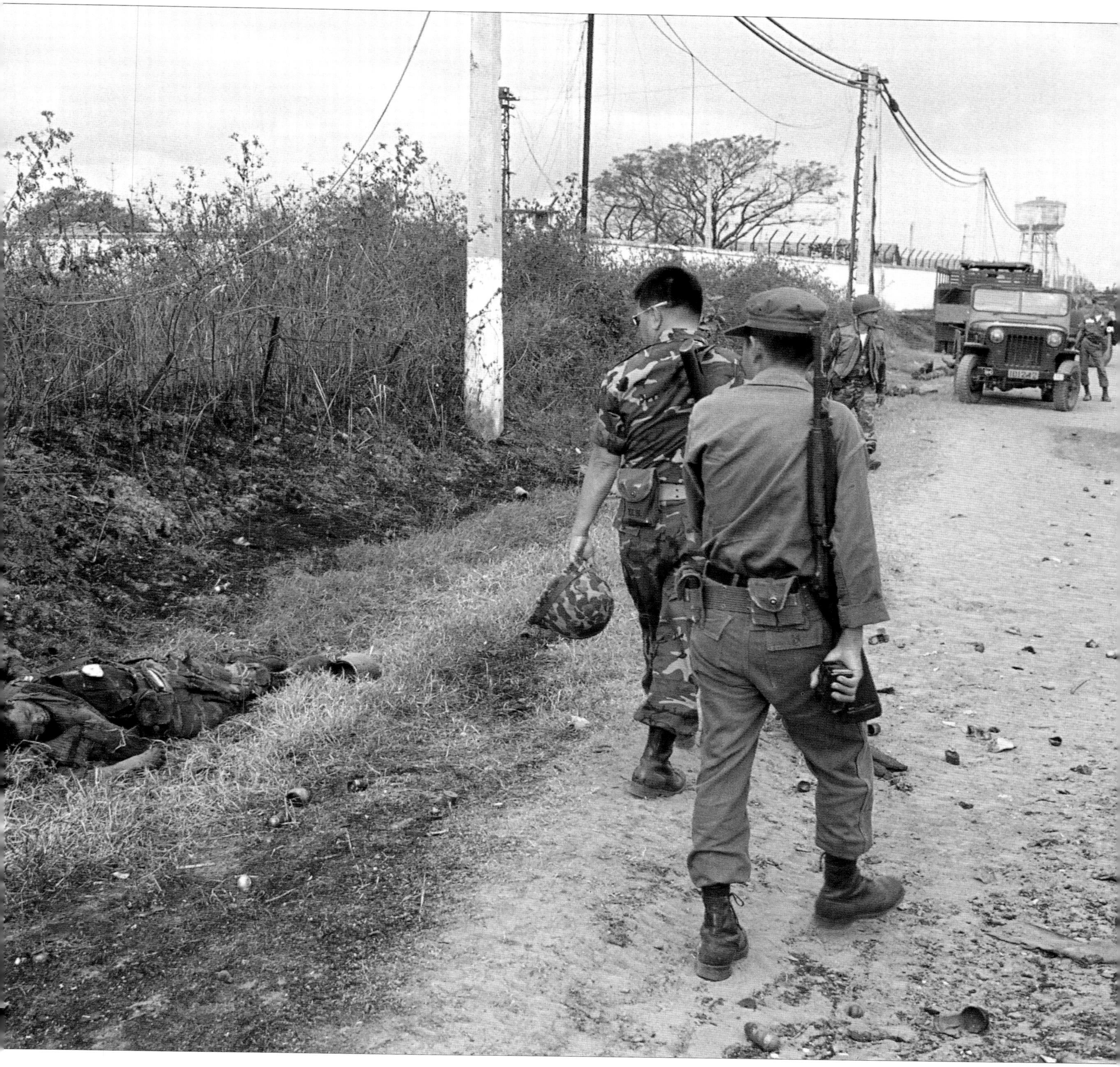

competent. Nevertheless, his request for reinforcements in the midst of the Tet crisis, while justifiable, was a public relations disaster. It delivered a psychological blow from which the American people never fully recovered.

◆ ◆ ◆

If guerrilla war is a clash of wills, how does one undermine the will of the insurgent? This is the classic question that faces the commander of the counterguerrilla force, a question few have been able to answer successfully. There are only three approaches to the problem: the first is to give the insurgents what they want, to co-opt their own program of reform, whatever that may be. The second is to isolate the guerrillas from their source of supplies—empty bellies and arsenals will drain the will of any force, no matter its motivation. The final and most brutal course is simply to kill enough insurgents to reduce their number to the point where they must accept defeat or face almost certain annihilation. Most successful antiguerrilla campaigns combine aspects of each approach. The least effective typically rely on the last.

A prime example is the Soviet Union's failed war in Afghanistan. In 1979, faced with an unstable client regime beset by a growing Islamic rebellion, the Soviet Union decided to install its own puppet government in Kabul, the Afghan capital. The only alternative appeared to be the emergence of a radical Islamic state in Afghanistan, a prospect viewed with alarm by the Soviets, who had their own restive Muslim population. Consequently, mechanized and airborne units left the Soviet Union and swept into Afghanistan in December 1979, overthrew the tottering Afghan government, and set up their own strongman, Babrak Karmal, to rule in its stead. While the coup was a spectacular success, the problem of the Afghan resistance did not disappear. In the early days of 1980, riots flared in virtually every Afghan city, and the countryside swarmed with bands of Afghan hill fighters, collectively known as mujahideen. Karmal's army melted away, many units deserting en masse and taking their weapons with them. If the Soviets wanted peace in Afghanistan, they would have to impose it themselves.

More easily said than done. From their mountain fastnesses, the Afghans have resisted invaders for millennia—no people are tougher or more inde-

The helicopter provided the American army with the mobility it needed to defeat the communists in battle after battle in Vietnam. It could not, however, win the war for the United States and its allies.

pendent guerrilla fighters. The communists were unwilling to accede to resistance demands, as the programs of the Soviet Union were antithetically opposed to those of the mujahideen. Nor could the communists interdict the mujahideen supply lines as they snaked through the mountains of the Hindu Kush to isolated base areas and into neighboring Pakistan. The Soviets and their Afghan allies instead resolved upon a murderous war of attrition, aiming to seek out and destroy the various mujahideen bands, one by one if necessary. In the spring of 1982, they launched their largest offensive of the war to wipe out 3,000 tribesmen led by the Soviet's canniest foe, Ahmad Shah Massoud.

Panjshir Valley

The enemy knew his terrain like the back of his hand.

—Soviet infantry officer

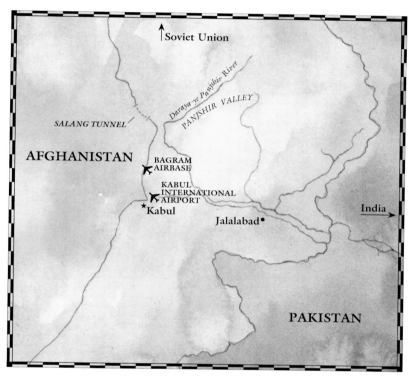

The valley drained by the Panjshir River is narrow and walled by mountains that soar straight up out of the ground. Canyons and side valleys branch off every so often, most of them rising rapidly into the highlands. The bottom land contains some of the most fertile soil in Afghan-istan; during the time prior to the war, some 150,000 people, most of them farmers, inhabited the 62-mile-long (99.2km) valley. Unfortunately, their native valley provided easy access to three targets of importance: the main communist air base at Bagram; the Salang Tunnel, through which Soviet reinforcements and supplies flowed; and Kabul. Thus, the Panjshir Valley became an avenue for mujahideen raids and the site of numerous Soviet operations.

Four previous offensives into the valley had failed to eliminate Massoud's resistance unit. In May 1982, nearly 15,000 Soviet and loyalist Afghan troops were mustered for a fifth attack. For one week, Soviet bombers pummeled the valley from end to end. These raids were not directed primarily at the guerrillas but at the civilian population, the purpose being to destroy crops in the field and depopulate the countryside. The strikes had little effect militarily, instead serving notice to Massoud that a major attack was imminent. The mujahed commander accordingly mined the roads, withdrew his men to the hills,

Top: Babrak Karmal, leader of the Soviet Union's puppet regime in Afghanistan. Above: The Panjshir Valley, a nest of Afghan resistance, pointed like a dagger at the heart of the Soviet occupation forces.

and called for assistance from neighboring resistance groups.

Communist artillery opened a preliminary barrage on May 17, 1982, covering the insertion of heliborne assault troops. Soviet gunships escorted Hip and Hook transport craft as they carried infantry and artillery into the valley and established a series of fire bases within the range of artillery at the western terminus. Mujahideen machine gunners posted on the hillsides ambushed many of the flights, often able to fire down upon the low-flying helicopters and scramble away before hovering Hind attack helicopters could swoop in to en-

gage them with rockets. By May 20, battalions of elite paratroopers occupied several choke points along the valley floor as tank and motorized rifle units opened a ground attack.

The Soviet strategists hoped that these fire bases would trap the mujahideen as the main column of mechanized units drove up the valley from west to east. This tactic, however, failed miserably. Massoud used his handful of mortars and captured artillery pieces to harass the bases, shifting his position constantly to avoid Soviet air and artillery. Meanwhile, the ponderous mechanized column ground its way up the valley, slowed by mines and repeated ambushes.

Typically, extensive barrages preceded the advance, often harmlessly striking empty positions while the Afghans chatted unconcernedly nearby. Then, as the lead communist units methodically swept the road for mines, the mujahideen hustled to their ambush site. The Russians preferred to lead with loyalist Afghan units, using them as bait—a tactic unappreciated by the already miserable Afghan conscripts. When the troops inevitably blundered into a mujahideen trap, Soviet armored forces moved up in support, attempting to catch the guerrillas in the open. The resistance fighters, however, rarely waited to be overrun, withdrawing quickly up the mountainsides or into the narrow, twisting side valleys where the Soviets'

Duds for Scrap

The Soviets and their Afghan allies dropped a huge number of bombs during the war in Afghanistan, but shoddy Russian workmanship produced a significant number of duds. Additionally, poorly trained Afghan pilots, in the excitement of combat, habitually neglected to arm their weapons. The result was a countryside littered with unexploded ordnance, which the resourceful mujahideen turned to their own advantage by extracting the explosive material for use against the former owners. Moreover, a cottage industry sprang up in the collection of duds and their resale for scrap. Caravans of bomb-laden mules often crossed into Pakistan, where dealers bought up the unexpected bounty. Needless to say, much of the profit was reinvested in the resistance effort.

tracked vehicles could not follow. Moreover, few Soviet infantrymen cared to dismount from their armored carriers to chase the nimble mujahideen along the precipitous ridges.

The result of each such engagement was a few casualties, perhaps a disabled tank or armored personnel carrier billowing smoke, and the tip of the column snarled in confusion. While the units sorted themselves out, artillery barraged the road ahead, and the process began all over again. As the column inched painfully forward in this manner, Massoud simply bypassed the fire bases along the high ground or allowed the column to pass him completely, in favor of an ambush of the vulnerable supply convoys that trailed behind it. When the ground units finally reached a fire base, the air assault troops leapfrogged farther up the valley, and the column set off once more.

From time to time, the Soviets scored a local success when some guerrilla leader, largely untutored in modern warfare and displaying more courage than sense, unnecessarily exposed his followers to the full weight of communist firepower. In the main, however, the campaign was an affair of skirmishes, with the increasingly frustrated Soviets unable to come to grips with any sizable body of resistance fighters. By June 13, the Russians had had enough, and the column reversed itself, withdrawing from the valley. As they pulled back, fields and villages were put to the torch, and mines were scattered liberally across the valley floor. The wrecked carcasses of thirty-five helicopters and more than fifty armored vehicles remained behind in mute testimony to the offensive's failure.

The fifth offensive in the Panjshir Valley demonstrated the utter bankruptcy of Soviet policy in Afghanistan. Tactically, the attempt to trap Massoud's band was clumsy in the extreme—despite great effort, fewer than 200 mujahideen were killed. Strategically, the widespread devastation and 1,200 civilian deaths merely hardened Afghan resolve and drove more men into guerrilla camps—exactly the opposite of the intended effect. Moreover, the attack failed to eliminate the Panjshir as an effective guerrilla base. Massoud's men returned to attacks on Bagram, Kabul, and the Salang Tunnel even as the offensive was winding down.

◆ ◆ ◆

Like the Spanish, French, and Americans before them, the Soviets had discovered the difficulty of hammering into submission an impassioned people; likewise, they had learned the cost of underestimating their enemy. Or perhaps they had not. In September 1982, Russian bombers returned to the Panjshir, heralding the sixth (but not the final) offensive into the valley. It was no more successful than its predecessors.

An Afghan resistance fighter fights back invaders with a heavy machine gun (which was undoubtedly captured from the Soviets or brought in by Afghan army deserters) amid the peaks of the Hindu Kush.

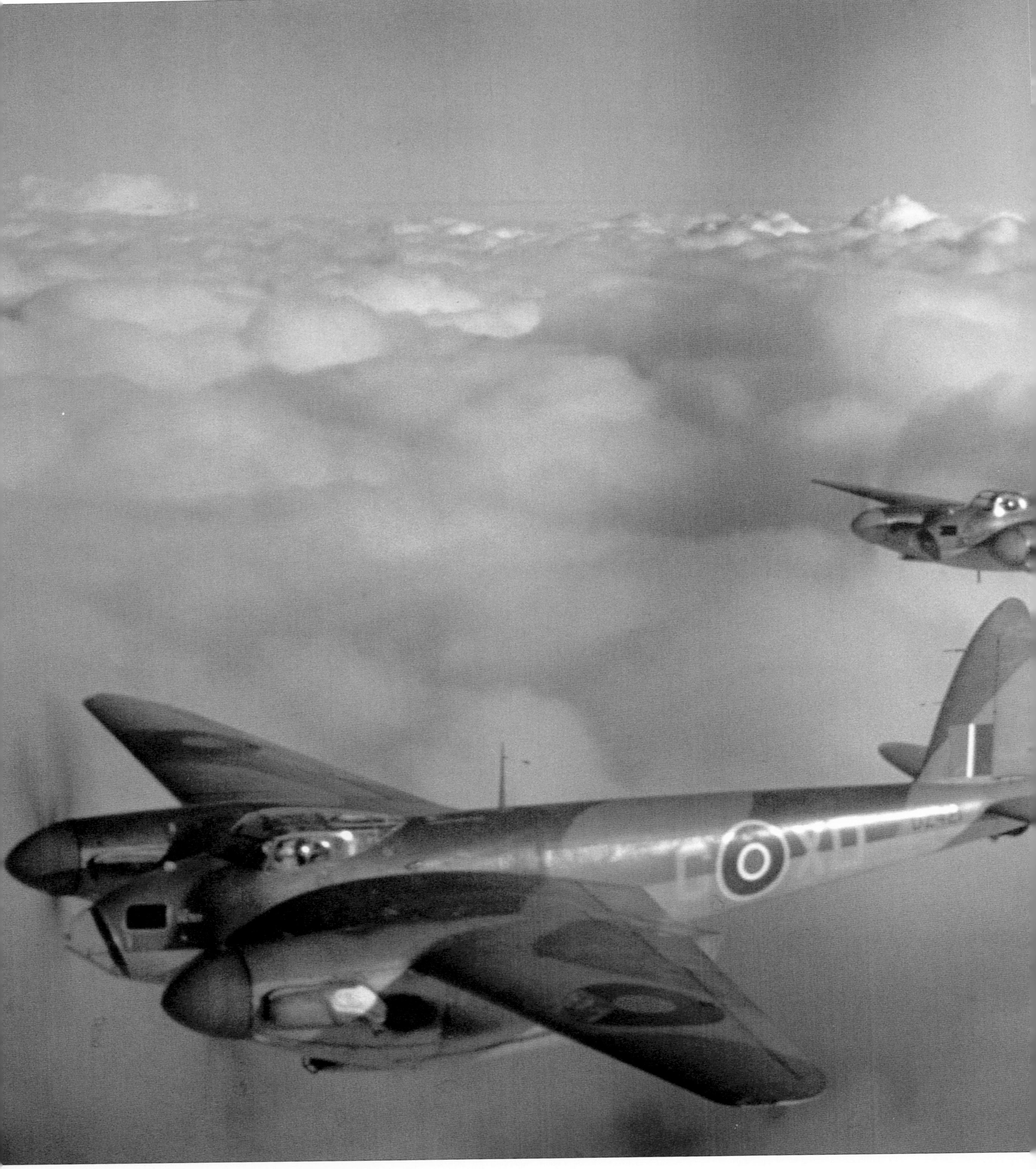

3

BATTLE OF BRITAIN • PLOESTI
SCHWEINFURT • ROLLING THUNDER

War in the Skies

Just over a decade after the Wright brothers' first flight, men were killing one another in an entirely new medium. By the end of the First World War, airplanes had explored almost every conceivable wartime role—reconnaissance, strategic bombing, aerial resupply, close air support, antishipping attack, and air-to-air combat; further air-war advancement wouldn't arrive until the advent of intercontinental ballistic missiles decades later. The planes themselves were primitive, and the tactics were developed through trial and error. Nevertheless, the promise of this new weapon fascinated military thinkers throughout the interwar years.

Some theorists, such as the Italian Giulio Douhet, believed that the advent of the warplane rendered armies and navies mere auxiliaries: wars would be decided within a few days by massive aerial fleets dropping bombs and poison gas on enemy cities. As it turned out, Douhet and his disciples put too much stock in the future capabilities of bombers (at least until the introduction of nuclear weapons) and seriously underestimated the ability of the civilian and industrial sectors to absorb punishment from the air.

But as World War II began, this truth was not yet clear. Belligerents armed with mighty bomber armadas strained to find the best way to apply this weapon against the enemy's war-making infrastructure. For the first time, armed forces could bypass the opponent's army or navy and strike directly at the enemy interior.

The first trial of this new type of war took place in the summer of 1940. Hitler's legions had subdued most of western Europe, invading and defeating Denmark, Norway, Holland, Belgium, and France. The British army had escaped the continent by the skin of its teeth, abandoning its heavy equipment on the beaches of Dunkirk. Only the Royal Navy stood between England and Hitler's planned invasion, code-named Operation Sealion. The German navy, however, stood no chance of defeating the much larger and more capable British Fleet.

But if Hitler's air force, the Luftwaffe, could gain control of the air over the English Channel, the Royal Navy could be driven off, leaving England open to invasion for the first time since 1066. In July 1940, the Luftwaffe began to probe the Royal Air Force (RAF), preparing an all-out offensive in August. It ultimately drove the RAF to its breaking point but failed to push it beyond because of one of the peculiarities of aerial warfare. In an environment in which ground cannot be seized or held, in which it is difficult to gauge the enemy's strength or the effects of bombing attacks, in which few prisoners are taken, how can the effectiveness of a campaign be judged?

A squadron of de Havilland Mosquitos heads for Germany in February 1943.

53

Battle of Britain

And so now we turn to England. How long will this one last—two, three weeks?

—Hermann Göring

London burned throughout the night of September 7, 1940. Three hundred German bombers had pummeled the city in the late afternoon, setting ablaze the slums of East London and the dockyards. While fire brigades struggled to contain the conflagration, Luftwaffe night bombers returned, adding their loads to the inferno. Thirteen hundred Londoners were killed or wounded that night, and thousands more were left without shelter.

The Royal Air Force's Fighter Command had not reacted well to the raids. Caught off guard by the scale of the strike against the British capital, it proved difficult to muster fighters quickly enough to hamper the German attack. Squadrons were fed into the air battle as they became available, and as a result, casualties had been heavy. Forty-two planes were lost, along with fourteen irreplaceable pilots.

But the man responsible for the aerial defense of Great Britain, Air Chief Marshal Sir Hugh Dowding, felt immensely relieved. A quiet man who stifled his emotions, he did not relish the suffering of the Londoners burned out or buried beneath the rubble of their homes. Nevertheless, he knew that the Germans had just lost the Battle of Britain.

The German aerial assault on Britain had begun in earnest on August 13 (code-named Adlertag, or Eagle Day, by the Luftwaffe). For the next three weeks, while invasion barges gathered in French and Belgian channel ports, an average of 1,000 planes a day roared over

Above: Though German bombers ranged as far afield as Belfast and Scotland, the majority of the action took place over the southeast of England—the aptly named "Hell's Corner."

southeastern England in a bid to destroy the RAF.

The British held several advantages in the contest. Radar stations along the coast detected German bombers as they approached, allowing Fighter Command to amass its aircraft against the invaders and reducing the need for wasteful air patrols. Ground observers aided in tracking the enemy as they proceeded inland, and highly efficient operations centers juggled squadrons from sector to sector as the need arose. The fact that most of the dogfighting took

place over England also allowed for a high rate of pilot recovery; conversely, when German aircrew bailed out, they were rendered prisoners of war.

The Germans, however, could muster far greater resources than could their British foes. Though they suffered heavily throughout the Battle of Britain, new planes and aircrew were readily available to fill the gaps. The RAF, on the other hand, had one great vulnerability: while British factories could generally turn out enough fighters to replace the planes they lost, fighter pilots were not so easily produced. RAF training wings needed time to teach young men the fine art of flying the Hurricane and Spitfire fighters in combat, but time was in short supply. At the height of the battle, even with an infusion of experienced—and vengeful—Polish, Czech, and French expatriates, the RAF was losing pilots at twice the rate of replacement.

Throughout the latter part of August and into September, the Luftwaffe conducted an unremitting campaign against the airfields of southeastern England. Dowding had little choice but to fling his scarce squadrons into the fray, for loss of these airfields would be tantamount to ceding the Germans air superiority over the channel, creating the conditions needed to launch Operation Sealion.

The raids destroyed repair facilities and planes on the ground, disrupted communications with Fighter Command headquarters, killed pilots in barracks and

London firefighters survey damage wrought by the Blitz. The dome of St. Paul's looms in the background.

Hermann's Mistakes

Hermann Göring was quite possibly the most incompetent leader of high rank in World War II. With few qualifications for command other than his skill at toadying to Hitler, Göring consistently derailed the German war effort by impulsively interfering in operations.

Besides his blunders during the Battle of Britain, he also allowed the British army to escape annihilation at Dunkirk in June 1940—ironically, by convincing Hitler that the Luftwaffe could destroy the British army on the beaches. Consequently, Hitler gave orders for the advancing panzer columns to halt for several days, providing the narrow margin that the English needed to evacuate their troops from defeated France. In 1942, he boasted to Hitler that the Luftwaffe could fly 600 tons (540t) of supplies a day into besieged Stalingrad—pure fantasy, considering the weather and the dearth of available transports—thereby convincing the dictator to hang on while breakout was still possible. The effort failed, and the German transport fleet was permanently crippled in the process.

Göring also neglected the development of new technologies such as radar and jet engines, and allowed his training facilities to deteriorate, largely through his unwillingness to grapple with such tawdry details when he could be hunting at his palatial estate outside Berlin. On the other hand, he tried to create his own private army by fielding Luftwaffe divisions to fight alongside the Wehrmacht, including a full-fledged armored division (appropriately enough, named the Hermann Göring Division). These formations were, with few exceptions, a waste of precious resources.

By 1945, with the Reich's cities in ruins, Göring may have been the most heartily detested man in Germany. Captured by the Allies and tried at Nuremberg after the war, he evaded punishment by committing suicide. His passing went unmourned.

in mess halls, and put landing strips out of action for days at a time. All these blows had a combined effect on the quality of the British response. Squadrons were slower to react to attacks, and ground support crews faced greater difficulties in putting damaged planes back in the air. Thus, the remaining Hurricanes and Spitfires faced a more difficult task in turning back or disrupting raids, which, of course, made the Luftwaffe's assault even more effective. As casualties mounted, Dowding was forced to rely on greener pilots, who often fell in their first encounter with German aces and their outstanding ME-109 fighters.

Still, the Germans were taken aback by the savagery of the aerial fighting between London and the coast. Constantly reassured by their own intelligence services that they had indeed broken the back of Fighter Command, the Luftwaffe aircrews nevertheless continued to fly daily into swarms of RAF fighters. They began calling the airspace Hell's Corner.

The crisis for Fighter Command intensified over the so-called Bad Weekend of August 30 through September 1. Every available fighter was rising to defend the airfields, but the pilots were approaching their last reserves of energy. Many flew four or more missions a day, and those shot down in the morning were stuffed back into a cockpit to fly later that afternoon. Exhaustion began to take its toll, and the kill ratios slipped to nearly one to one, an unsustainable rate of exchange for the British. Moreover, several important airfields lay wrecked and smoking. Privately, Dowding calculated that his men could sustain such a pounding for another week, two at the most. Then the fighter squadrons, or what was left of them, would have to be withdrawn to north of London.

But just as the RAF was on the verge of defeat, the corpulent figure of Hermann Göring intervened. A First World War ace addicted to morphine, fine art, and gluttonous living, Göring had risen to command the Luftwaffe largely on the strength of being an old crony of Hitler. Impatient and distrustful of his subordinates, Göring understood little about modern air warfare. The continuing resistance of the British infuriated him, as did a minor nuisance raid against Berlin by English night bombers.

Feeling pressure from Hitler to bring the Battle of Britain to a rapid conclusion and to retaliate for the Berlin raid, Göring called a conference at The Hague in occupied Holland for September 3. There, he made a fateful decision that he believed would kill two birds with one stone: with Hitler's support, Göring decreed a suspension of the

A Luftwaffe gunner peers out the nose bubble of his bomber, searching for approaching British fighters.

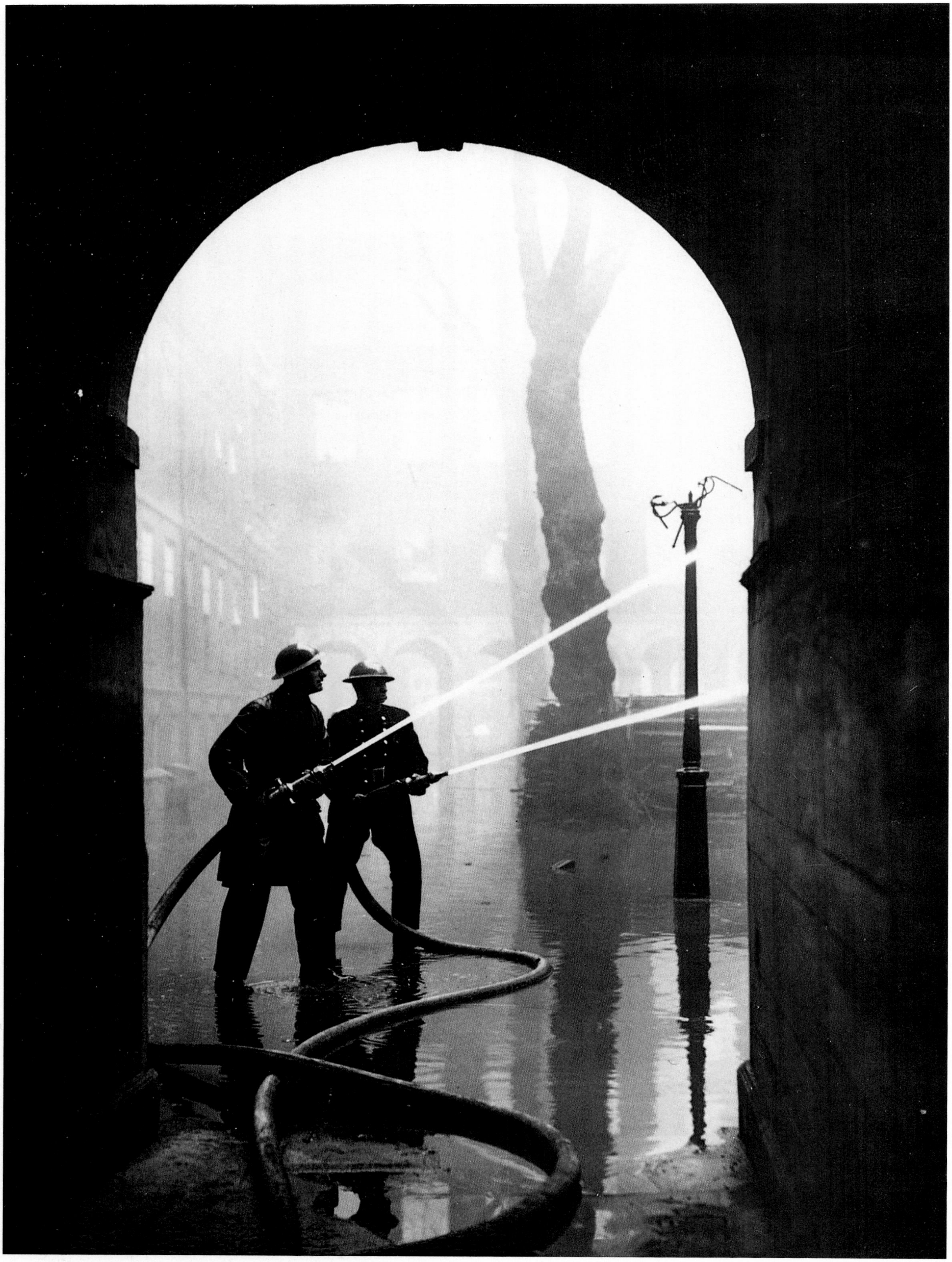

airfield bombing and ordered his bombers to turn against London itself, beginning on September 7. He anticipated drawing Fighter Command's last reserves into the skies over London and destroying them there. After that, continued strikes against the city would soon break civilian morale, forcing the English to sue for peace.

Despite the success of the initial attack, the change in tactics proved disastrous. By taking the pressure off the airfields, Göring offered Dowding the respite he so desperately needed to revitalize his command. Moreover, the effort to bomb London during daylight hours broke the back of the Luftwaffe. London was too far away from the German-controlled French airfields for the short-winded ME-109s. Their fuel capacity allowed them to loiter for only about ten minutes over London, after which they had to leave the bombers to continue unprotected. A daily slaughter ensued, as the RAF's Spitfires and Hurricanes roared in virtually unopposed.

During the daylight hours of September 15, Göring hurled his bombers against London once more. He hoped the attack would finally sweep the British from the sky and allow Operation Sealion, now tentatively scheduled for September 27, to proceed.

His hopes were dashed. Fifty-one bombers—a quarter of the force that was flying that day—crashed to the green English countryside. No air force could long survive such a loss rate, and further daylight raids against the city were called off. Though night raids continued well into 1941, they steeled rather than eroded British resolve and in themselves were an admission of defeat.

The RAF had turned back the Luftwaffe and retained control of the air over the channel, but only because Göring did not have the patience to follow a successful course of action to its conclusion. He had hoped the assault on London would force the British into a conclusive battle, but the truth was that Dowding had only one target that he felt forced to defend: his airfields. He could choose to respond to raids on London at a level that allowed him to rebuild his shattered fighter reserve, and this was what eventually tipped the balance in favor of the RAF.

✦ ✦ ✦

By 1943, the Allies had turned the tables on the Germans. Large fleets of British bombers, often accompanied at least part of the way by fighter plane escorts, struck at the Third Reich during the night, while the Americans chose to pursue a strategy of daylight bombing. The benefits of daylight strikes included easier coordination of formations and more accurate bombing, but flying during the day also resulted in heavier casualties.

The Americans believed that the best way to bring the Nazi war machine to a grinding halt was to select vital portions of its industry and concentrate strikes against those. One obvious candidate was the oil industry. Germany relied on only a very few sources of petroleum to fuel and lubricate its machinery; if these could be knocked out, everything from factories to planes to the dreaded panzers would be crippled. The problem lay in the nature of the targets. The destruction of pumping stations, pipelines, refining towers, and the other paraphernalia of petroleum processing located deep within the continent—beyond fighter escort range—required extreme accuracy.

Left: The bombing of London destroyed entire sections of the city, but failed to break British morale. Above: The Hurricane fighter was one of the greatest tools of the tenacious defenders during the Battle of Britain.

Ploesti

You should consider yourself lucky to be on this mission.

—Major General Lewis H. Brereton

O n August 1, 1943, several B-24 Liberators of the American Ninth Air Force began to drop beneath the cloud cover blanketing the Wallachian Plain of Romania. The heavily laden bombers were on the final leg of a journey from Benghazi, Libya, to the huge oil-producing center of Ploesti. Their mission was to destroy the complex of storage tanks, refineries, and processing plants that supplied Nazi Germany with a third of her petroleum products.

Major General Lewis H. Brereton, commander of the Ninth Air Force, had chosen to attack Ploesti at treetop level —an unorthodox and dangerous tactic, but the only way that he believed his bombers could achieve the pinpoint accuracy necessary to cripple the Third Reich's refining capacity. Intelligence reports indicated that Ploesti was lightly defended by a few obsolete Romanian fighter squadrons and fewer than 250 antiaircraft guns, most of them small-caliber weapons. The eighty or so heavy-flak guns would be unable to track the bombers as they flashed by at low altitude.

The attack would be mounted by five bomb groups, each disposing about thirty-five bombers. Taking off from Benghazi, the groups would observe radio-listening silence during the long flight in to avoid detection and then hit the various targets in and about Ploesti in carefully coordinated waves. The first bombers were armed with delayed action bombs so that the following waves would not be distracted by explosions as they hurtled in low and fast. With any luck, the strike would be over and the bombers away before the dazed Romanians could mount an effective defense.

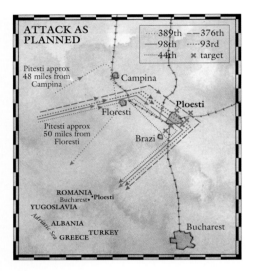

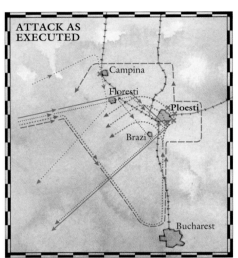

Top: Major General Lewis H. Brereton (shown here early in his career) had as much wartime experience with bombers as any other U.S. airman. Above: The bombing runs over Ploesti were designed to maximize surprise and striking power—but the plan quickly came unglued as a result of mischance and human error.

On paper, the plan looked good, but things began to go awry over the Mediterranean. At dawn, 178 B-24s, swollen with full bombloads and extra fuel tanks, lumbered into the air, but by the time they reached the Adriatic coast near the island of Corfu, thirteen had already crashed or returned to base because of mechanical failures. The planes containing the mission's lead and deputy navigators were among the missing, and the job of navigating for the entire bomber stream had fallen on the shoulders of a young lieutenant named William Wright.

As the groups rose to cross the mountain ranges of Albania and Yugoslavia, Axis ground observers alerted the Luftwaffe high command; the enemy now knew that a large force of bombers was on its way, though they did not yet know its destination.

Over the mountains, variable winds pushed two of the groups far ahead of the others, bucketing through heavy weather at a slightly lower altitude. Unable to keep in visual contact and forbidden to use the radios, the bombers had dropped out of the clouds over Romania in two separate waves. The first consisted of the 376th and 93rd Bomb Groups; the second, following well behind, contained the 98th, 44th, and 389th Bomb Groups.

By now, the two prerequisites for success outlined in Brereton's plan— the element of surprise and a quick, coordinated attack—were rapidly slipping away. Within a few minutes of the planes' descent, the prerequisites would disappear altogether.

The 376th and 93rd had leveled off at an altitude of 500 feet (150m) and were approaching the small town of Floresti, just 13 miles (20.8km) northwest of Ploesti. Floresti was a landmark for the navigators, the point where the bombers would bank south-

The Surprise after Pearl Harbor

Everyone knows of the devastating surprise attack on Pearl Harbor. On the morning of Sunday, December 7, 1941, Japanese carriers launched an attack that sank the U.S. Pacific Fleet at its moorings and propelled America into the Second World War. Unbelievably, the Japanese were able to repeat their performance against the U.S. Far Eastern Air Force stationed at Clark Field in the Philippines.

The B-17s and fighter aircraft had scrambled into the air that morning upon hearing the news from Pearl Harbor, but after flying around for some time without spotting any Japanese invaders, they returned to Clark Field. Planes were refueled and parked carelessly, almost as if the crews had forgotten there was a war on. Shortly afterward, Japanese raiders screamed in low over the horizon and destroyed nearly all the planes on the ground. How the attackers managed to evade detection is not entirely clear, but this "second Pearl Harbor" made flaming wrecks of seventeen bombers and fifty fighters and eliminated at a single stroke the only Allied airpower stationed between Singapore and Hawaii.

east to make their final run into the target area. Unfortunately, the second plane in the formation contained the mission commander, Brigadier General Uzal Ent. Ent was undoubtedly aware of the inexperience of Wright in the lead plane, so when Ent mistakenly identified the wrong town as Floresti, he did not hesitate to order his pilot to turn to the southeast—prematurely. The lead Liberator and its young navigator continued on the correct course, but the rest of the 376th and the 93rd followed their commander toward Bucharest, the Romanian capital.

Many other pilots recognized the error, but bound by the strictures of radio-listening silence (by now a useless precaution), they could only gnash their teeth and remain in formation.

Over Bucharest, Ent finally realized his blunder and turned the groups toward Ploesti, but the flight over the city alerted local defenders, dashing any remaining hopes of surprise. Moreover, the 93rd and 376th would now be ap-proaching Ploesti from the south instead of the northwest, making the task of finding targets even more difficult.

It was a flight into hell. The antiaircraft guns around Ploesti, now fully manned and ready, were serviced not by Romanians but by crack German crews. Furthermore, the defenses included 240 of the deadliest flak guns of the war, the lethal "88," many of them cleverly hidden in haystacks, fake buildings, and railcars. Deployed in concentric circles, the 88s were fully capable of hitting the Liberators even as they hugged the ground for safety. Supplementing the big guns were hundreds of lighter artillery pieces.

Planes began to fall long before the targets were reached. Among the first, ironically, was William Wright's, its nose smashed by a single flak burst. But as Liberators cartwheeled into the earth, the survivors pressed on at 50 feet (15m) or less above the ground, the fire intensifying as they reached the outskirts of the city.

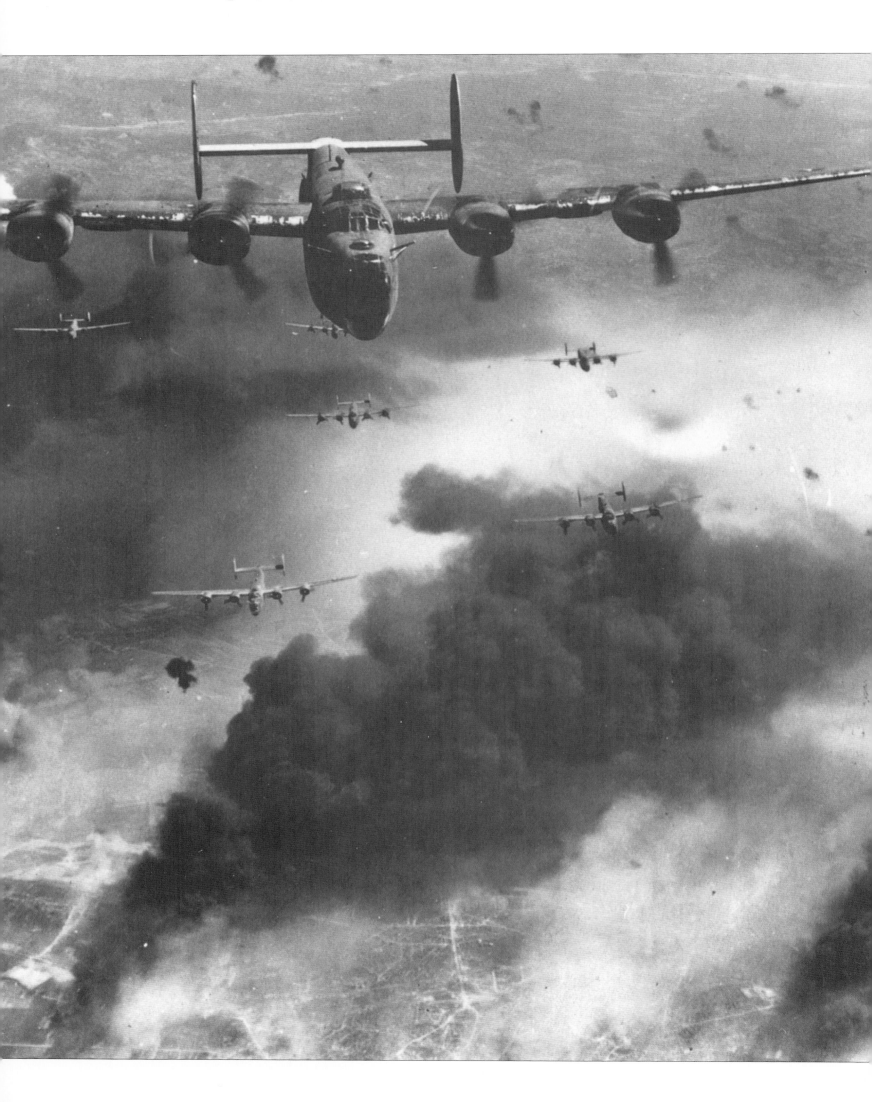

Coming in from an unfamiliar direction, pilots and navigators strained to spot their targets, dodging barrage balloons, chimneys, and bridges. Unable to find his primary target, the commander of the 93rd—his plane ablaze—led his men to an alternate one. The commander's B-24 suddenly plunged into the earth, but the following planes managed to dump their loads. The Liberators of the 376th likewise struck targets of opportunity before veering away toward home.

The remaining three bomb groups swept over the target area just as the remnants of the 93rd and 376th were trying to claw their way out. By now, the sky over Ploesti was thick with black smoke, making the avoidance of obstacles more a matter of luck than of skill. Pilots in the 44th and 98th Groups also had to contend with the unexpected appearance of their comrades from the first two groups, now scattered and flying in any direction that promised escape. Planes collided in the murk, further disrupting the attack. Sheets of flame shot up from burning tank farms or delayed-action bombs, engulfing several of the low-flying bombers as they made their runs. And always, the flak guns hammered away, shredding wings, fuselages, engines, and men.

Finally, the last planes limped away from Ploesti, but the airmen's travails were not yet over. Brereton had promised that they would face only Romanians in mediocre fighters, but the planes that flashed down to riddle the ragged American formations as they straggled homeward were expertly handled Luftwaffe ME-109s. The enemy concentrated on

A spectacular sight—a tight formation of B-24 Liberators over Romania.

As for Ploesti, while it did suffer considerable damage, none was permanent. Although production dipped about 40 percent for a short time, within the space of a few months it had not only recovered but increased.

◆ ◆ ◆

The raid on Ploesti was a perfect example of a plan gone awry because of too many working parts. Its dependence on surprise, fair weather, close coordination, and weak opposition violated one of warfare's ironclad principles: all else being equal, simplicity works best. When human error was added to the mix, disaster resulted.

In comparison, the American strategic bombing campaign mounted from England against Germany was almost brutal in its simplicity: rugged bombers bristling with machine guns and flying in closely packed formations for mutual support were hurled against the Third Reich. In theory, the bomber's defensive firepower, combined with sheer weight of numbers, would blast through the defending fighters and hammer the target into rubble.

Beginning in 1942, the Americans probed deeper and deeper into the continent, until planners felt confident in their ability to strike factories in the very heart of enemy territory. They were disabused of this notion in late 1943 by the aerial equivalent of Pickett's Charge.

those planes that were too crippled to keep up with the rest, hounding them unmercifully until they crashed into the Romanian countryside. Their fuel running low, the fighters turned away at last.

Exhausted and bloodstained crews struggled to keep the wounded Liberators aloft for the 1,300-mile (2,080km) journey back to North Africa. Of the 164 planes that had made it to Ploesti, forty-one had been brought down by the enemy or had simply disappeared in the chaos over the city. Two more collided on the way home, with no survivors. Of the 121 remaining planes, eight landed in neutral Turkey and were interned, and twenty-three more landed at Allied bases elsewhere in the Mediterranean. Only ninety touched down at Benghazi, fewer than three dozen of which would ever fly again. The aircrew toll was also high: of 1,726 crewmen in the raid, 310 died and more than 230 were wounded, captured, or interned.

Above: Brigadier General Uzal Ent (far right), who was known as the "Flying General," kneels to discuss the mission with his pilots before takeoff. Below: A remarkable photograph of a Liberator in flight over Ploesti, just moments after releasing its deadly cargo.

Schweinfurt

Our navigator has an easy job today. All he has to do is follow the trail of burning Fortresses and parachutes from the task forces ahead of us.

—U.S. bomber pilot

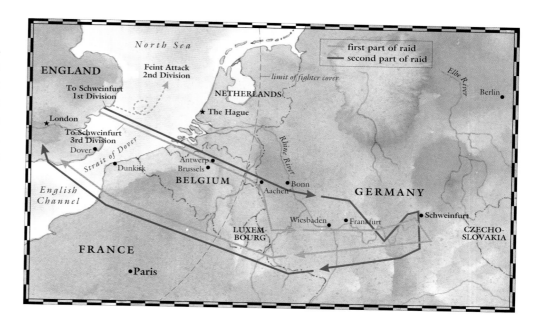

All across southeastern England, the crewmen of seventeen bomb groups waited for the signal to abort or proceed with Mission 115. Low clouds scudded over a countryside shrouded in fog, but skies were clear over Germany. Green flares were arced up to announce that the Schweinfurt Raid was on. Within minutes, the first bombers were taking off, looking like ghosts as they disappeared into the mist. It was October 14, 1943, forever after known to the men of the Eighth U.S. Air Force as Black Thursday.

Sixty B-24 Liberator and 291 B-17 Flying Fortress bombers were scheduled to attack the ball-bearing plants at Schweinfurt, an industrial town in the heart of the Third Reich. This was the second attack on the German city, the first having taken place in August, and the bomber crewmen consoled themselves with the thought that this mission could not be more difficult than the last, when nearly forty bombers were lost. They were wrong.

Misfortune plagued the bombers from the start. None of the Liberator groups were able to participate, as inclement weather prevented them from effectively forming up. Mechanical difficulties forced twenty-six B-17s to turn back to England; as a result, only 265 bombers actually crossed the Dutch coast.

The Flying Fortresses were successful in linking with their escorts—P-47 Thunderbolts from the 56th and 353rd Fighter Groups. The fighters tangled almost immediately with Luftwaffe ME-109s and FW-190s as the attackers entered enemy airspace. With few ex-

Unlike Ploesti, the Schweinfurt raid was brutally simple—but the target was simply too deep and the Luftwaffe too strong.

ceptions, the Thunderbolts held the interceptors at bay, but the American fighters could remain with their charges only as far as the ancient German city of Aachen, where they were forced to turn back for lack of fuel.

As the P-47s peeled away, the Luftwaffe unleashed its most savage attack of the war. In 1943, the Luftwaffe defense forces were operating at peak efficiency; for the Schweinfurt raid, they coordinated and massed their attacks with such precision that the sky around the Fortresses was never empty, except over the city itself, where German antiaircraft fire took over. The German pilots, experienced but not yet decimated by losses, had also developed effective tactics in dealing with large formations of bombers. They had learned to attack

head-on where the Fortresses had the most difficulty in concentrating their formidable firepower, and they focused their attacks on one group at a time. Once that group was sufficiently shot up, the fighters moved on to the next, systematically dismantling the protective "boxes" that the American airmen worked to maintain.

The Luftwaffe had also introduced several new air-to-air weapons, including aerial bombs designed to explode in the midst of a bomber group and rockets that were far more frightening than dangerous as they roared erratically through the sky. Nevertheless, it was the traditional fighters that posed the greatest threat to the B-17 crewmen as they struggled across western Germany.

With their fighter escort gone, the B-17s suffered a merciless pounding. During the 200-mile (320km) trek from Aachen to Schweinfurt, ceaseless Luftwaffe attacks spun thirty-seven bombers out of formation and into the

Precision Bombing

In late July 1944, while the Allied armies in France were stymied in their efforts to break out of the Normandy beachhead, it was proposed that heavy bombers be used to saturate (or carpet-bomb) a select portion of the German lines. Planners envisioned American troops pouring through a gap blasted by 1,600 Fortresses, Liberators, Marauders, and Invaders.

Unfortunately, it is much more difficult to distinguish targets along the front lines than it is to pick out a factory or rail yard. On July 24 and 25, the bombers swept in over the German entrenchments—at least, most of them did. Many bombardiers, unable to locate the enemy positions with any certainty, bombed so far to the German rear that they had little effect; others inadvertently attacked a friendly forward air base and completely destroyed an American ammunition dump. One group mistakenly unloaded over American units, killing 136 and wounding 440 troops of the U.S. 30th Infantry Division. Among the dead was the highest-ranking American officer ever killed in action, Lieutenant General Lesley McNair, commander of Army Ground Forces, who was on an inspection trip from Washington, D.C. He had wanted to observe the effect of the carpet-bombing.

unyielding German earth—an average of one plane lost every five miles (8km).

Over the city itself, while the German fighters returned to their bases to refuel and rearm, flak began to explode in dirty black puffs. The antiaircraft fire was designed more to distract bombardiers during the final bomb run than to actually knock down planes, but periodically a B-17 lost a wing or snapped in half as a burst found its mark. Remarkably, despite their recent ordeal and the thick ground fire, the bombers delivered their loads accurately, inflicting significant damage on the factories below.

As soon as the planes turned back toward England, they faced another trip through a gauntlet of enemy fighters.

The survivors closed up ranks, and the stragglers went down quickly. Weary gunners wrestled their machine guns around to face wave after wave of interceptors as the bombers lumbered toward Holland and the protective embrace of waiting American fighters. By the time they reached their escorts and relative safety, twenty-three more bombers had been lost.

Still, the danger had not entirely passed. Crippled bombers with engines out or landing gear missing had to be landed, often by pilots weak from loss of blood. Five planes were so badly damaged that the crews bailed out over England rather than risk a landing; seventeen others touched down but would never fly again. Of the 200 bombers that returned, only sixty had survived without any damage.

The raid on Schweinfurt had cost the Eighth Air Force eighty-two bombers and more than 600 crewmen, a loss rate of nearly 30 percent. Though Nazi ball-bearing production—so vital to virtually every aspect of their war industry—had been damaged, another week's worth of casualties on such a scale would have destroyed the Eighth Air Force's bomber groups. The massacre

over Schweinfurt led to a suspension of deep daylight raids until a long-range fighter could be developed to accompany the bombers throughout their attack and wrest control of the air from the Luftwaffe. Courage had not been lacking—not a single pilot aborted once over Germany, and several planes were seen conducting their bomb runs while on fire—but the American leadership had asked for more than its men could deliver.

◆ ◆ ◆

The only sustained strategic bombing campaign launched since World War II was the American effort over North Vietnam. The planes were bigger, faster, and had more powerful weapons, but the military problem was the same as in the 1940s: how best to use airpower to force one's enemy to submit. The strategy chosen by the administration of Lyndon Johnson proved to be the wrong one.

Above: This photograph of bomber crewmen after a raid was probably staged. Few crews returned from any raid, especially Schweinfurt, so cheerful and unscarred. Left: By 1943, the American industry was turning out huge numbers of bombers, but the loss rate suffered over Schweinfurt— nearly 30 percent—was still unsustainable.

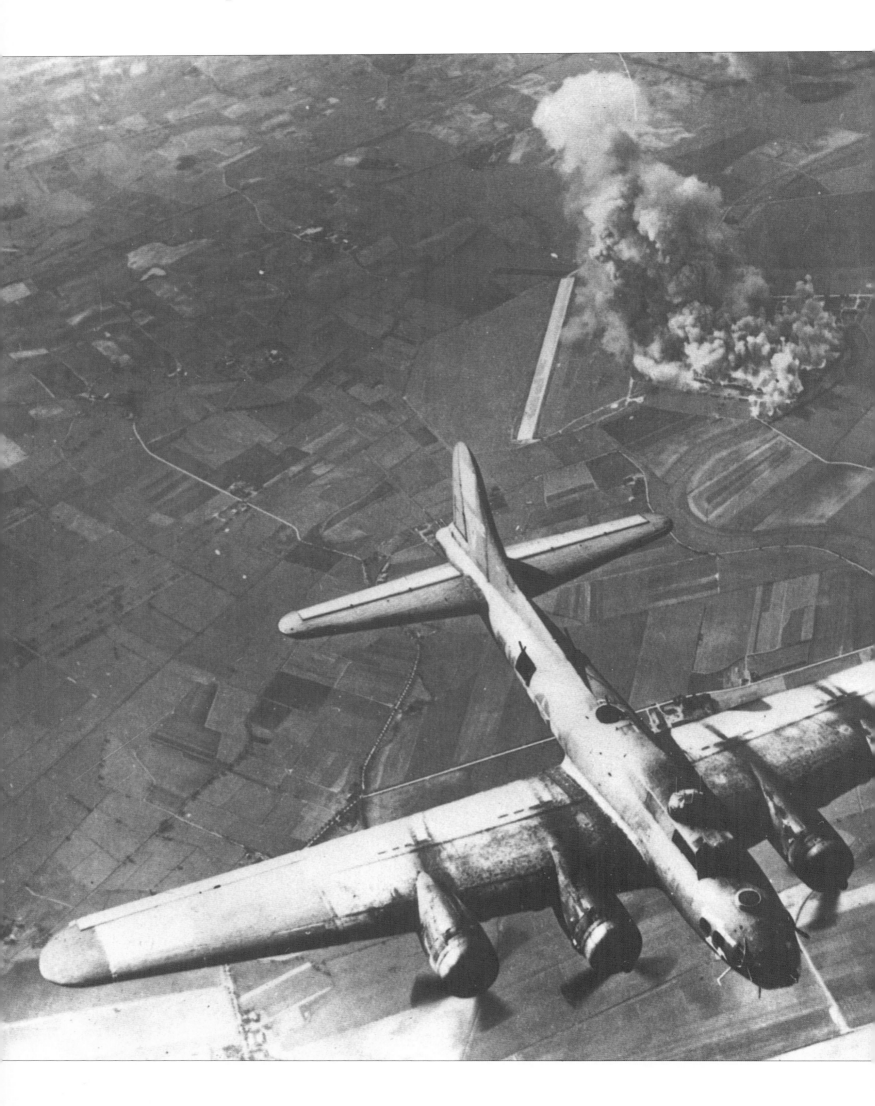

Left: A B-17 Flying Fortress making its way through the German skies. Below: Bombs drop toward their target. The Americans chose to make bombing runs during the day, believing that the increased accuracy was worth the increased risk. Note the bombers flying in formation at the top of the picture.

Rolling Thunder

I fear that, to date, Rolling Thunder . . . has merely been a few isolated thunder claps.

—Maxwell Taylor, U.S. Ambassador to South Vietnam

Above: America's bombing campaign against North Vietnam suffered from politically imposed restraints, a resourceful enemy, and the world's strongest air defense system.

On March 2, 1965, more than 100 planes lifted off from fields in South Vietnam, Thailand, and Okinawa. Winging over North Vietnam, they attacked and destroyed an ammunition dump at a loss of only five aircraft. This signaled the beginning of an operation that continued fitfully for the next three years. This campaign was code-named Rolling Thunder and its purpose was threefold: to interdict the flow of men and material from the north to the communists operating in Laos and South Vietnam, to destroy the primitive arms industry in North Vietnam, and, most important, to punish the north for its support of the Vietnamese War and force its leaders to the conference table.

The Joint Chiefs of Staff planned a classic campaign: first destroying ports and the transportation net, they would then proceed to bludgeon depots, factories, and oil plants, while ancillary raids suppressed North Vietnamese airfields and antiaircraft batteries.

But President Johnson and his civilian advisers, particularly Secretary of Defense Robert McNamara, had other ideas. Enamored with academic theories about war and diplomacy, McNamara wanted a campaign of slowly mounting intensity. Supposedly, the North Vietnamese, who realized that the screws were tightening and who were eager to avoid future punishment, would accede to negotiations. This notion of limited bombing corresponded with Johnson's desire to hold down costs and avoid any deeper involvement in Vietnam than was absolutely necessary.

As a result, the execution of Rolling Thunder was bound by politically motivated restrictions. First, no possible excuse would be provided for Chinese or Soviet intervention; thus, Haiphong, North Vietnam's principal port of entry for Soviet and Chinese ships, was off limits, as were any targets within 30 miles (48km) of the Chinese border. Second, to avoid world censure, civilian casualties had to be kept to an absolute minimum; therefore, the heavily populated regions around Hanoi were also off limits. Third, distrustful of the military's judgment, advisers in Washington required that all targets be approved in advance so that no untoward incidents would interrupt the steady march toward political settlement.

Changes to the target list were considered, and largely rejected, at lunchtime conferences attended by Johnson, McNamara, adviser Walt Rostow, and the presidential press secretary. No military officers were permitted to attend these meetings, where timing of raids, numbers of planes, and even tactics were sometimes decided, until late 1967. Finally, the bombing was halted every so often, with peace feelers extended to see if the North Vietnamese had had enough.

But the communists were strangely reluctant to relent. And no wonder, for the airpower of the world's strongest nation made little impression on Hanoi's will to continue the war.

Although individual strikes proved lethal enough, the target list rarely contained enough important sites to impede the southward dispatch of supplies. The list published in July 1967, for instance, allowed strikes against only six-

allowed the northerners to repair damage to industry and infrastructure or to disperse plants and storage facilities around the country. Most significant, the ban on raiding or mining Haiphong harbor permitted a free flow of war materials from the outside world, rendering U.S.-inflicted damage to the north's industries largely moot.

On the tactical side, frustrated pilots often watched Vietnamese MiG fighters rising to engage them, though they were unable to interfere because their airfields lay within prohibited territory. The stereotyped tactics, routes, and targets forced upon the American fliers allowed the North Vietnamese to concentrate the densest array of modern antiaircraft weaponry—including the latest surface-to-air missiles (SAMs) —against the navy and air force bombers who were conducting Rolling Thunder. By New Year's Day of 1966, after a thirty-seven-day bombing halt, the north had emplaced 2,000 antiaircraft guns and fifty-six SAM sites, all manned and ready to repel raids.

Rolling Thunder proved a failure on all counts. The lack of a systematic attack on the road and rail network, coupled with the ban on attacking Haiphong, ensured that northern support of the war would continue. (For example, despite steadily mounting sorties over the north, infiltration of soldiers southward rose from 35,000 in 1965 to 90,000 in 1967.) The north's industry was crippled several times, but pauses in the campaign allowed it to be rebuilt or at least relocated, and production invariably recovered. And finally, though U.S. planes dropped more tons of high explosives on North Vietnam than had been dropped on Germany in all of World War II, the bombing failed to shake Hanoi's will to continue. Ironically, Rolling Thunder did more to undermine American support for the war, as a wave of protest arose to demand the cessation of bombing. The spectacle of American bombers over North Vietnam, finely played by the communist propaganda machine, turned many Americans into opponents of Johnson's war effort.

Secretary of Defense Robert McNamara tours South Vietnam in 1967. A brilliant academic, McNamara was hamstrung by his misunderstanding of the use of force.

teen of the 274 targets around Hanoi and Haiphong that were considered by the military to have high payoff. Vital bridges and rail yards sometimes dropped inexplicably from the list, mistakes that allowed the North Vietnamese time to repair them. Bombing halts also

Rolling Thunder's creators did not survive the campaign. McNamara resigned in early 1968, his scheme for bringing the war to a conclusion in ruins; Johnson decided not to run for reelection, so unpopular had his policies become. Hope died hard, however. Sensing that Hanoi was yet again ripe for negotiations, Johnson ordered the final suspension of Rolling Thunder on November 1, 1968. Four days later, Richard Nixon was elected president, and the communists were busily repairing their airfields, bridges, and roads.

The failure of Rolling Thunder, which cost the United States more than 1,000 planes during its forty-four months, became all the more tragic when eleven days of unrestricted bombing of Hanoi and Haiphong in December 1972 brought the north to its knees and its diplomats to the conference table.

Above: A4 Skyhawks attack the Thanh Hoa Bridge in late 1967. A vital link in the road network from north to south, this bridge was attacked repeatedly during Rolling Thunder. Right: In early 1968, bombs fell on a North Vietnamese Army barracks. This was one example of the poor target selection that plagued Rolling Thunder.

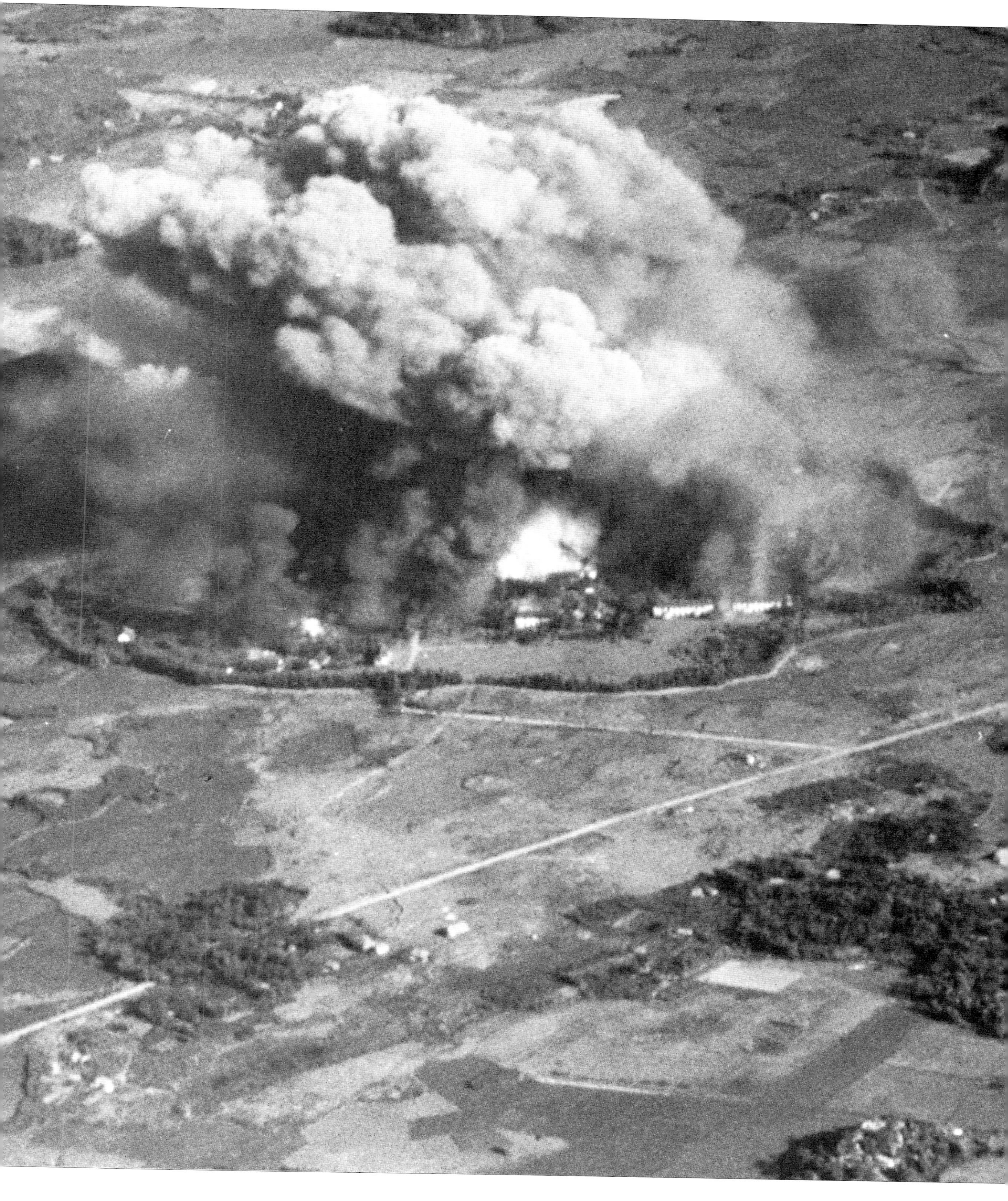

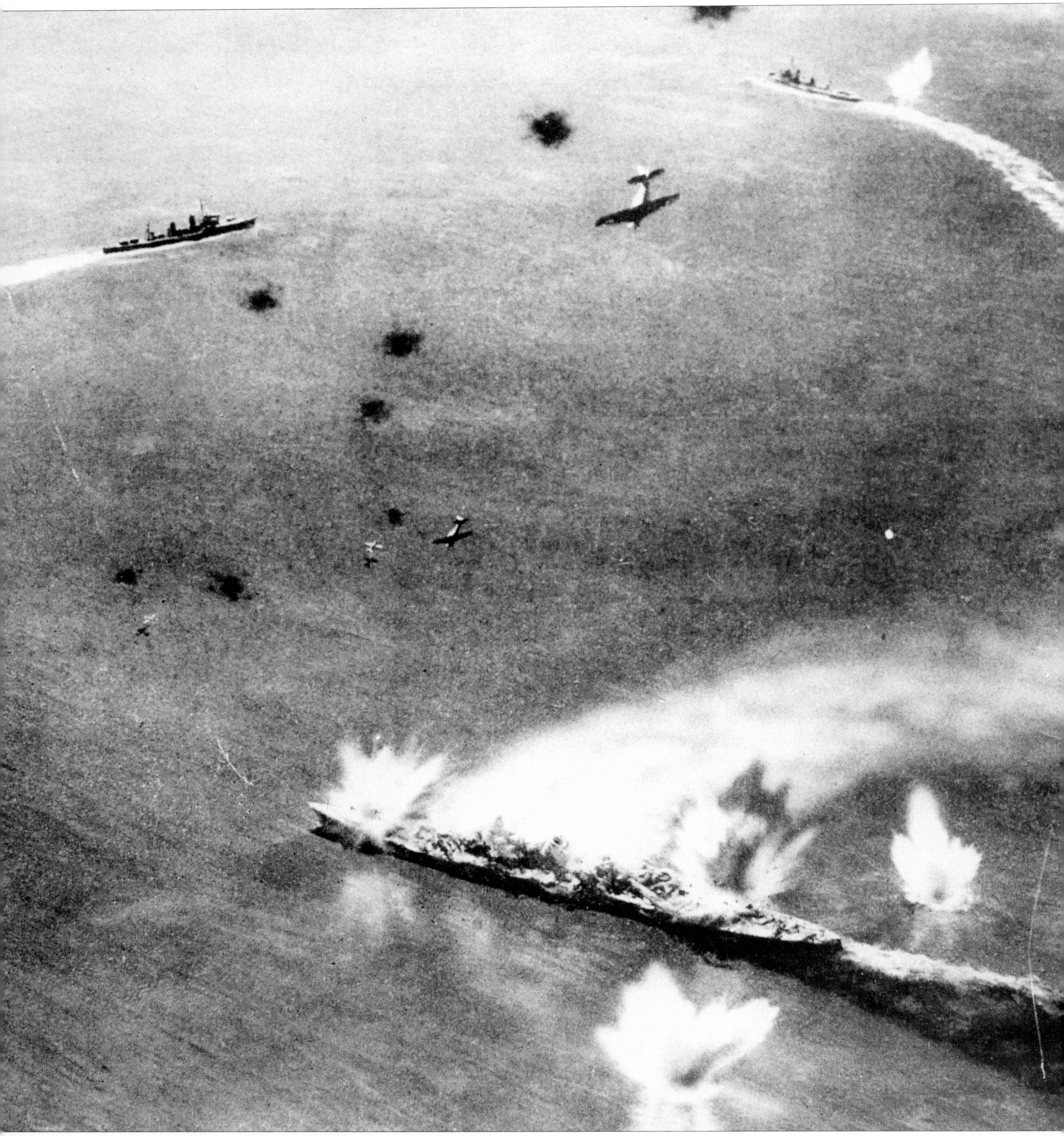

4

TSUSHIMA • MIDWAY
OPERATION DRUMBEAT • PQ-17

War at Sea

It is said that the army equips men, while the navy mans equipment. This reveals a fundamental difference in commanding on land and commanding at sea. Every sailor on a ship, in essence, services a single weapon, and that weapon is controlled directly by the ship's captain. On land, each soldier controls his own weapon, while the commander ensures that each individual uses his weapon to best effect. Moreover, while land forces often operate autonomously from the will of the commander, the sailor, enclosed by steel walls, has little choice but to respond to that will.

This is not to discount the the human spirit's role in naval warfare—sailors often display a courage that surpasses understanding. Rather, it emphasizes the fact that the tactical skill of the commander is of paramount importance during a sea fight, for unlike land combat, talented subordinates can rarely overcome the effects of an admiral's or a captain's blunder.

The tempo and risks of naval warfare vastly exceed those of land warfare. War at sea is brutal, violent, and short. Opportunities come and go rapidly, and commanders are directly exposed to the consequences of their mistakes. Furthermore, the environment is inherently hostile; man cannot live for long in the water, and in some places, once exposed to the elements, his life expectancy can be measured in minutes.

These special pressures have produced some spectacular blunders during this century. At a higher level of operations, two new weapons, the aircraft and the submarine, have extended the sphere of operations both above and below the water.

Before going into the effects of new weaponry, however, let us start with what may be considered the last of the "classic" naval blunders, which occurred in the restricted waters between Japan and Korea. Throughout the nineteenth century, the Russian and Japanese empires had been expanding into northeastern Asia, and by the turn of the century a clash had become inevitable. In 1904, war broke out over the issue of which empire would dominate and exploit Korea and the Chinese province of Manchuria. In retrospect, it seems inevitable that vigorous, reform-minded Japan would triumph over corrupt, incompetent czarist Russia, especially as the latter had to operate so far from its source of supply and manpower in Europe. But at the time, many thought it inconceivable that a major Western power could be defeated by an Oriental, non-Caucasian country. Japan's victory at Tsushima, therefore, marked the dawning of a new world order. It is ironic, then, that the battle itself would have been familiar in form to any eighteenth-century sailor.

Dive-bombers from the USS Hornet *attack Japanese ships during the Battle of Midway.*

Tsushima

Defeat is a common fate of a soldier. There is nothing to be ashamed of in it.

—Admiral Togo to Admiral Rozhdestvenski,
a few weeks after the battle

In June 1905, expectant crowds lined the quays of Vladivostock, imperial Russia's last naval base in Asia. These people awaited the arrival of the Second and Third Pacific Squadrons under the command of Rear Admiral Zinovi Rozhdestvenski, fleets that represented Russia's last hope for victory in the war against Japan. Since the war's eruption in February 1904, the Japanese had captured Port Arthur (the premier Russian naval base on the Pacific) after an epic siege, virtually destroyed Russia's Pacific fleet, landed hundreds of thousands of troops in Korea, and driven the czar's armies deep into northern Manchuria. The only chance of salvaging the situation lay with Rozhdestvenski's ships: if the fleet could reach Vladivostock after its nearly 20,000-mile (32,000km) journey from European waters, it might then be able to sever Japan's lines of communications over the Yellow Sea and the Sea of Japan. If Rozhdestvenski could accomplish that, the Japanese armies in mainland Asia would wither on the vine, and the territory lost in the past year might be regained.

Thus, when the cruiser *Almaz* appeared on the horizon, the spectators cheered lustily. But the excitement died away as it became apparent that the *Almaz* sailed alone. The battered cruiser's crew brought news that further dampened the crowds' spirits: the remainder of Rozhdestvenski's fleet was gone, save two destroyers that would

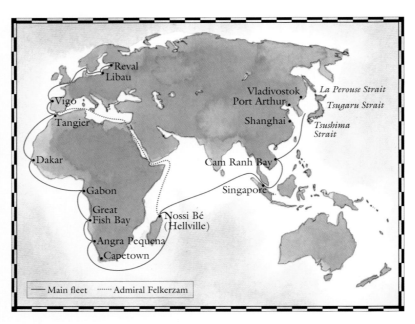

Top: The ill-fated Admiral Zinovi Rozhdestvenski upon his departure from Kronstadt. Above: The Baltic Fleet's voyage to the Pacific, which began in Russia in October 1904, was an epic adventure in itself, but it ended in disaster as the Russians tried to force passage through the Tsushima Strait in May 1905.

limp into port sometime later. After a seven-month journey across half the globe, the Russian squadrons had been destroyed in a single afternoon.

The journey had begun in October 1904, when the Baltic fleet departed Kronstadt, the great naval fortress that guarded Saint Petersburg. Fifty ships sailed, including seven battleships, seven cruisers, and nine torpedo-armed destroyers; the fleet also included smaller escorts, a hospital ship, an icebreaker, supply transports, and even ships for refrigerating food and condensing potable water from the ocean.

Almost from the first, the fleet—now named the Second Pacific Squadron—was beset with difficulties. Many of the vessels were cranky old tubs, prone to breakdowns that slowed progress to a snail's pace. The inefficient imperial bureaucracy was unable to maintain a steady flow of supplies to the ships, forcing Rozhdestvenski to suffer interminable waits in neutral ports along the way. Especially infuriating was the consistent delay in obtaining fuel for his coal-fired ships.

On November 3, the Russian ships reached Tangier. Some of the older vessels were dispatched through the Suez Canal, while the rest of the fleet passed out of European waters and embarked on the long loop around the southern tip of Africa. As the ships labored down the west coast of Africa, tropical heat and diseases began to afflict the crews. Already demoralized by tyrannical and brutish discipline, bad food, and mind-numbing boredom, many sailors jumped ship, committed suicide, or simply went mad. Nevertheless, Rozh-destvenski drove his command relentlessly, rounding the Cape of Good Hope in mid-December. After weathering a fierce hurricane, the two halves of the Second Pacific Squadron reunited on Christmas Day at the aptly named port of Hellville, on the island of Madagascar.

There Rozhdestvenski received news that reinforcements were on their way from Russia, in the form of a Third Pacific Squadron. He was to wait at Hellville for the eight to ten weeks that

The Battle of Dogger Bank

Shortly after leaving the Baltic Sea but long before they reached Tsushima, the Russian fleet fought a one-sided battle near the Dogger Bank, a shallow spot in the North Sea. For some reason, rumors had spread throughout the fleet that Japanese submarines and torpedo boats were lying in wait just off the coast of Denmark. However unlikely this may have seemed, considering that Japan was more than 18,000 miles (28,800km) away by sea, orders went out that no unidentified ship was to be allowed near the fleet; all crews were placed on alert. Around midnight on October 17, a Russian auxiliary ship reported that she was being chased by "eight or nine" torpedo boats, a report accepted unblinkingly by the staff on Rozhdestvenski's flagship. About an hour later, with nerves throughout the fleet keyed up by this sighting, firing broke out as the Russians found themselves in the midst of forty to fifty 100-ton (90t) ships. For about twenty minutes, the Russians fired indiscriminately, sinking several of the shadowy boats and managing to fire into one another on at least two occasions.

By the time they got their panicky gun crews under control, the Russian officers discovered to their horror that the "enemy" was in fact part of an English fishing

fleet, innocently plying their trade in international waters. Dozens of fishermen were killed or wounded, some as they waved haddock to try to identify themselves to the Russian battleships. The ugly incident nearly precipitated hostilities between Britain and Russia, especially after the czar expressed his regret but refused to apologize. Eventually, passions cooled, and Russia paid compensation to the families of those killed or wounded and replaced the sunken trawlers.

---

it would take for the support squadron to arrive. The enforced idleness proved disastrous. The wretched French colonial outpost offered little to enliven the men's existence; its waters were shark-infested and foul from the fleet's refuse; and the temperature hovered in the high nineties (high 30s C). Drunkenness ran rampant, uniforms hung in tatters, and mutinies exploded on several ships because of the poor quality of the food. Only the arrival of a mail boat from Russia—the first contact from home in four months—averted an all-out revolution. Even the normally hearty Rozhdestvenski grew haggard and ill; the admiral may have suffered a minor stroke at Hellville, and his left leg now dragged noticeably.

Finally, Rozhdestvenski resolved to sail before his fleet rotted at anchor. Departing on March 17, the Russians completed a nearly 5,000-mile (8,000km) trip across the Indian Ocean, reaching

Singapore on April 8. On May 9, the Third Pacific Squadron at last joined Rozhdestvenski at Cam Ranh Bay in French Indochina. Shortly thereafter, the combined Russian fleet weighed anchor and set off on the last leg of its journey to Vladivostock.

Meanwhile, the Japanese navy, commanded by the redoubtable Vice Admiral Heihachiro Togo, awaited the Russians' arrival. Togo had gathered his forces to meet the Russians in Tsushima Strait, the narrow stretch of water between Japan and the southern tip of Korea, which afforded the most direct access to the Sea of Japan and Vladivostock beyond. However, farther north were two other entrances to the Sea of Japan: the Tsugaru Strait between the Japanese islands of Honsho and Hokkaido, and a more indirect route around the northern tip of Japan. Togo had deliberately left these unguarded, believing it unlikely that his foe would

risk either passage. However, heavy seas and fog hid Rozhdestvenski's approach, and as days passed without contact, the Japanese commander began to wonder if his Russian counterpart might be trying an end run.

Fortunately for Togo, Rozhdestvenski's first blunder gave away his intentions. On May 25, with Togo half-convinced that the Russian fleet had opted to avoid Tsushima, news came that Rozhdestvenski's colliers had arrived at Shanghai. The Russian admiral had sent off his precious coal freighters to protect them from harm during the coming battle, but by doing so, Rozhdestvenski had tipped his hand—he would have needed the colliers for resupply if he intended to sail through either of the northern entrances to the Sea of Japan.

Thus, when the crew of an armed Japanese merchant ship spotted the Russian fleet in the early morning hours

Above: Admiral Togo on the bridge of his flagship. The Japanese consciously modeled their navy on the British fleet, down to the cut of their uniforms. Right: The Russian battleship Borodino *shortly before she capsized with the loss of all hands save one. Togo's fleet can be seen in the background.*

of May 27, Togo's ships were still in position to intercept. Later that morning, the Japanese cruiser *Izumi* detected the Russian squadrons sailing northward in two columns. The *Izumi* shadowed the enemy fleet and relayed its position to Togo via the newfangled wireless telegraph.

By 9 A.M., the Russians were passing the southern end of Tsushima Island as Togo's fleet bore down on them from the north. Rozhdestvenski's twelve battleships steamed in two columns, eight in the westernmost and four in the eastern; nine cruisers and eight destroyers protected the flanks of the main battle line. Unfortunately, Rozhdestvenski neglected to use his lighter ships as scouts, so he sailed in complete ignorance of Togo's location, heading, or formation. Thus, when at 1:19 P.M. the Russians emerged from a fog bank and the two fleets sighted each other at last, they were unprepared, whereas Togo had already formulated a plan of attack. The Japanese raced south in a single column, six battleships in front, trailed by six armored cruisers. A swarm of destroyers and torpedo boats supported the battle line.

Rozhdestvenski eyed the approaching Japanese from the bridge of the battleship *Suvarov*. As he watched, Togo's column turned to starboard, still out of range but closing fast. The Russian admiral judged that Togo wanted to race down his port side to mask the fire of Rozhdestvenski's easternmost column while he pounded the western column. Accordingly, he ordered his squadrons to form a single column so that all guns could be trained on the Japanese as the two fleets passed each other. It was a fatal miscalculation.

Togo had no intention of simply slugging it out, broadside to broadside. Instead, he suddenly signaled his ships

to turn hard to port in succession, and the Japanese battle line began to wheel ponderously toward the head of the Russian column. The two opposing admirals, both at the head of their respective battle lines, now approached each other virtually at right angles. For a few minutes, Rozhdestvenski still might have reacted by turning away from or parallel to Togo's line, but the Russian admiral merely angled slightly to port to close the range. The *Suvarov* opened fire first, as most of the Japanese battleships were still circling to port, but the superior speed of the Japanese ships and the poor gunnery of the Russian crews allowed Togo to complete his maneuver and, for all practical purposes, win the battle almost before he fired a shot.

Within twenty minutes of his final turn, Togo had accomplished the tactical feat dreamed of by generations of naval captains—he "crossed the T." In other words, the entire Japanese battle line sailed across the front of the Russian column. This allowed the full weight of the Japanese broadsides to focus on one or two ships or to rake the entire column. The Russians, in contrast, could return fire only with their forward guns, and ships in the rear of the column were unable to fire at all. Consequently, the Russian battle line soon became a shambles. The *Suvarov*, the *Oslyabya*, the *Alexander III*, and the *Borodino* all began to burn, with the *Oslyabya* going down at 2:45 P.M. The Russian battleships that followed were wallowing in confusion, while destroyers darted in to pick up survivors. Togo's battleships, having crossed the T, turned again to work over several

Above: The Japanese sail into Vladivostock at war's end. Opposite: Admiral Togo in full panoply.

Russian ships that were attempting to flee northward, while the cruisers systematically blasted at point-blank range the flaming wrecks of those left behind.

The Russian crews hung doggedly at their posts, displaying exceptional bravery, if not great skill. The battle soon became a confused affair in the heavy seas and thick clouds of black smoke. The *Suvarov* sank at 7 P.M., her last gun still firing as she disappeared beneath the waves. The *Borodino* turned over and exploded soon after, with only one crewman surviving. The *Alexander III* went

down as the Japanese capital ships withdrew, leaving the Russians to the destroyers and torpedo boats.

As darkness fell, the nightmare continued. The Russian fleet had broken up by this time into wandering groups of fugitives, out of touch with one another and desperately seeking escape from the prowling Japanese. Rozhdestvenski lay wounded and unconscious in a badly leaking destroyer, having been evacuated from the *Suvarov* before she sank. Daring attacks by torpedo boats—running in so close that the Russian guns

could not be depressed sufficiently to engage them—sank two more battleships and crippled others so badly that they had to be scuttled. Japanese destroyers hunted down and dispatched any smaller stragglers.

By dawn on May 28, the last sizable group of Russian ships still afloat had been sighted by the returning Japanese battleships. This miserable remnant was pounded unmercifully until the white flag was hoisted to end the Battle of Tsushima. By day's end, all twelve Russian battleships had been sunk or captured, along with five cruisers and six destroyers. Three additional cruisers escaped the carnage, only to be interned at Manila in the Philippines, then an American possession. Togo had lost a grand total of three torpedo boats.

After their arduous 20,000-mile (32,000km) journey, the Russians had been destroyed just 300 miles (480km) short of their destination. The psychological and material blow to the Russian war effort was so great that the czar immediately turned to the United States as a mediator to bring the disastrous war to a close. A treaty signed in September 1905 handed Japan dominance over Korea and Manchuria and relinquished all Russian outposts in China, thereby fueling the expansion of the Japanese empire, an action that ended only with World War II. Czarist Russia, on the other hand, was left humiliated, impoverished, and wracked by revolution.

As for Rozhdestvenski, he survived to return to court-martial and disgrace in Russia. Ironically, it was his drive and determination that had dragged his fleet around the world to its doom; had he won at Tsushima or even avoided defeat, it is likely that he would be remembered as one of the century's great admirals. Instead, a series of errors at the very end of his epochal voyage led him into ambush at

Tsushima—and the worst defeat in modern naval history.

◆ ◆ ◆

Thirty-six years later, Japan faced only one remaining competitor in the Pacific —the United States. Resolving once more to stake her claim to hegemony through war, Japan struck hard at the United States Pacific Fleet at Pearl Harbor on December 7, 1941. In a plan masterminded by Admiral Isoroku Yamamoto, Japanese naval forces damaged or sank every ship in Pearl Harbor via surprise air strike. Unfortunately for the Japanese, no American aircraft carriers were in port that Sunday morning, leaving a dangerous counterweight to Japan's imperial ambitions alive in the Pacific.

Yamamoto resolved in early 1942 to eliminate this threat. By threatening the island of Midway, a lonely American outpost situated between Japan and Hawaii, Yamamoto hoped to lure the American carriers into a trap. A picket line of submarines would detect the Americans as they sallied forth from Pearl Harbor to defend Midway from invasion; it would also guide in Japanese aircraft from the 1st Carrier Force to smash the remainder of the U.S. Pacific Fleet. With their carriers gone, the Americans would have little choice but to remain on the defensive for another year and possibly sue for peace.

This time, however, the Japanese strategy failed. American cryptographers had broken the Japanese Purple code, used for supposedly secure naval transmissions, and were therefore well aware of Yamamoto's intentions. Two U.S. carrier task forces departed Pearl Harbor days before the Japanese submarines took up their scouting positions, and they lay in wait north of Midway. In the first days of June 1942, it was the Japanese who sailed into ambush.

Midway

Hell-divers!

—Japanese lookout aboard the *Akagi*

Vice Admiral Chuichi Nagumo, his broad shoulders hunched and his face impassive beneath his peaked cap, brooded aboard his flagship, the Japanese aircraft carrier *Akagi*. The morning of June 4, 1942, promised good visibility and fair seas, but Nagumo paid little heed to the weather for the moment. He had a decision to make, and he was not a man who enjoyed making decisions under pressure. Earlier, 108 planes from his four carriers (besides the *Akagi*, Nagumo's 1st Carrier Force included the *Hiryu*, *Soryu*, and *Kaga*) had bombed the American base at Midway Island. Bombers remaining behind had been heavily armed with torpedoes and dive bombs, ready to smash the American fleet should it make an appearance.

At 7 A.M., the flight leader had signaled that the results of the raid had been disappointing and advised Nagumo that another strike was needed to complete the destruction of the airfield on Midway. Nagumo hesitated to order such an attack for three reasons. One, he knew that he had been sighted by at least one American Catalina patrol plane, and therefore he had to assume that the Americans had at least a general idea of his position. Two, he did not know where the American fleet was or if there were any enemy carriers within range. Three, renewing the attack on Midway

Top: Ironically, the inherently conservative Admiral Chuichi Nagumo is best remembered for his ill-advised risk-taking at Midway. Above: After crippling the U.S. Pacific Fleet at Pearl Harbor, the Japanese sought to destroy the last American striking force, her surviving aircraft carriers, by luring them into battle near Midway Island.

would necessitate unloading all the torpedoes from the planes on the *Akagi* and *Kaga*—they were utterly useless against land targets—and replacing them with conventional bombs. This would be a time-consuming task on the crowded carriers, especially as the first wave would soon have to be recovered, with many planes damaged and all of them low on

fuel. On the other hand, the picket line of Japanese submarines between Midway Island and the American naval base at Pearl Harbor had not reported any sightings of enemy surface vessels, which probably meant that the American fleet still lay two or three days away. But the cautious Nagumo did not discount the possibility that the Americans had slipped past the picket line unnoticed.

As the indecisive Nagumo mulled over these factors, American planes finally appeared over the 1st Carrier Force. A handful of Marauder and Avenger torpedo bombers bore down on the Japanese, but since they lacked fighter escort most of the American planes were shot down by the nimble Zero fighters covering Nagumo's ships. The few bombers that survived were blasted out of the air by antiaircraft fire or forced to release their torpedoes at such a great distance that their targets easily avoided them. Not a single Japanese ship was damaged.

Apparently, the feebleness of the attack convinced the conservative Nagumo that it was safe to proceed with a second strike against Midway. All the attacking planes had been land-based; this implied that no American carriers were lurking nearby. Accordingly, he issued the fateful order to rearm the bombers on the *Akagi* and the *Kaga* with high-explosive and incendiary bombs. It was the first of his mistakes that June morning.

Deck crews on the two carriers hastily brought the planes below the flight deck to change out their armament. This work was proceeding when a Japanese scout plane reported ten enemy ships steaming toward 1st Carrier Force at a distance of 240 miles (384km). At 8:20 A.M., the scout radioed that at least one American carrier was present with the aforementioned ships.

Nagumo now thought that he must switch targets once again. Orders went out to the sweating armorers to replace the torpedoes. In their feverish haste to comply, crews did not return the conventional and incendiary bombs immediately to magazines belowdecks but left them stacked in the crowded hangars. Meanwhile, the fighters circling aloft—and still fending off occasional ineffective sorties from Midway—had to be landed and refueled, along with the planes now returning from the morning's first strike. The Japanese carriers became hives of activity.

By 9:30 A.M., all the returning planes had been recovered. Each of the carrier's hangar decks was crammed full of planes, bombs, and fuel, and flight crews worked amid a tangle of hoses, damaged aircraft, and armaments racks to ready the second wave for its attack against the American fleet. It was at this point that Nagumo committed his second blunder by ordering the 1st Carrier Force to turn toward the American fleet. What Nagumo needed now was time to clear his flight decks, restore a modicum of order to the chaos below decks, and reduce the vulnerability of his fragile carriers. Instead, by turning toward the enemy, he shortened his margin of error and brought himself closer to the American planes, which, unbeknownst to him, were now winging their way toward his ships.

Shortly before 10 A.M., the first groups of American bombers—obsolete Devastator torpedo planes—appeared at wave-top level; Zeros screamed down to intercept. The resulting air battle replayed the earlier encounter: with the American squadrons coming in uncoordinated waves, the Zeros were able to deal with the attackers in easily di-

gestible chunks. Thirty-six of forty-one Devastators pinwheeled into the sea, one by one, and the five remaining were unable to score a hit. The fighter assault was lethally effective but poorly controlled—eager to come to grips with the enemy, none of the fighters remained aloft to deal with a high-altitude attack.

As the slaughter continued, Nagumo's second wave of bombers assembled on the four flight decks. By 10:15 A.M., 102 were ready to launch, and the Japanese admiral gave permission for them to begin takeoff.

At this point, it appeared that a Japanese victory was assured: Midway had been hit hard, at least one American carrier had been sighted and marked for destruction, and several air attacks had been beaten off without Nagumo's precious carriers suffering a scratch. But five minutes later, the Japanese had not only lost the Battle of Midway—they had lost the war.

In those fateful minutes, the Japanese paid the price for the whole series of errors leading up to the battle's culmination: the failure of the submarine picket line to catch the American fleet as it moved northward days before; Nagumo's decision to switch from torpedoes to

By the time the Yorktown *suffered this crippling hit from a Japanese bomber, the outcome of the Battle of Midway was already decided.*

The Yorktown *lists heavily before sliding beneath the waves.*

conventional bombs for a second strike on Midway; his order to head for the American fleet before his second wave was ready; the carelessness of the flight crews in improperly stowing the high explosives and incendiaries as they were removed; and finally, the headlong plunge of the Zeros to dispatch the American torpedo bombers, which stripped the 1st Carrier Force of overhead fighter cover.

It was from overhead that fifty-five Dauntless dive bombers, launched from the carriers *Enterprise* and *Yorktown*, suddenly screamed down on the helpless Japanese. Only a smattering of antiaircraft fire popped around the American bombers as surprised gun crews struggled to elevate their weapons. The Zeros clawed frantically for altitude, but the attack had come too swiftly for them to interfere. Nagumo and his staff watched in stunned disbelief as the Dauntlesses scored hit after hit on the *Kaga*, *Akagi*, and *Soryu*. Bombs penetrated the teeming flight decks and slammed into the crowded hangars below. Fuel, explosives, and readied aircraft ignited instantly, transforming all three carriers into blazing hulks. As the last of the Dauntlesses pulled away at 10:30 A.M., only the *Hiryu* remained unscathed, her sisters all mortally wounded and burning uncontrollably.

The *Hiryu* managed to launch an attack against the American carriers that crippled the *Yorktown* so badly that she had to be abandoned later in the day. This was small consolation for the Japanese, for the *Hiryu* was hit in turn at 5 P.M. and scuttled early the next morning, completing the destruction of the 1st Carrier Force.

The Japanese navy never recovered from Midway. Forty percent of its carrier strength had been destroyed, along with hundreds of irreplaceable naval aviators. With new American carriers coming down the slipways every month, the balance of power in the Pacific had been permanently transformed.

◆ ◆ ◆

War with Japan had also brought America into conflict with Nazi Germany. The first naval battle of that war was fought just off the American coast, and unlike the daylong fight at Midway, it dragged on for nine months. Why it did so is a testament to the perversity of human nature as expressed through its institutions. If Tsushima was the last "classic" naval blunder, the American antisubmarine campaign of 1942 might be called the first "bureaucratic" blunder. Like so many products of modern bureaucracy, it was petty, protracted, and, for the most part, deadly dull. Unless, that is, you happened to be aboard one of the merchantmen stalked by German U-boats that deadly spring.

Operation Drumbeat

The trouble is, Admiral, it's not only your bloody ships you are losing. A lot of them are ours.

—British naval officer to a visiting American admiral

The United States had been at war for only three weeks when the German undersea fleet unleashed its first offensive against the east coast of North America, an operation code-named Paukenschlag ("drumbeat" in German). For nearly nine months, the U-boats ranged the Caribbean, the Gulf of Mexico, and the length of the eastern seaboard, slaughtering merchantmen. Though fewer than a dozen submarines participated at any one time, the average monthly loss of shipping just off American shores hovered at just over 300,000 tons (270,000t); in May 1942, Operation Drumbeat accounted for nearly 85 percent of Allied merchant marine losses. The pickings were so good that grinning U-boat men dubbed the first half of 1942 "the happy time."

The U.S. Navy did not sit idly by during this time; indeed, a great deal of effort went into the fight against the submarine menace. Nevertheless, the navy failed miserably for nearly a year in suppressing the wolf packs, driving them away from American shores only late in the autumn. This defeat is all the more remarkable in light of the navy's own antisubmarine experience of World War I and the hard-earned expertise of its British allies, who had been battling Nazi U-boats for over two years. The failure was so complete, and the scope of the disaster so great, that no single individual could be blamed. The poor performance against the U-boats re-

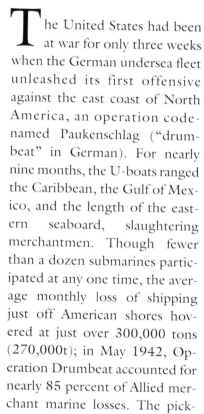

Top: Admiral Adolphus Andrews fought America's first naval campaign of World War II. Above: During World War II, the Germans conducted an incredible U-boat campaign along the North American seaboard, one of their happier hunting grounds.

sulted from a series of blunders spread over many years, often committed not by an individual commander but by the bureaucracies that had come to exert so much influence over warfighting in the modern age.

The story begins long before the war, as the U.S. Navy began a belated rebuilding program in the late 1930s. Admirals preferred to purchase battleships, aircraft carriers, and cruisers rather than less glamorous convoy es-

corts or antisubmarine patrol planes. The transfer of fifty destroyers to the Royal Navy in 1940 further depleted the inventory of Anti-Submarine Warfare (ASW) ships. As a result, Admiral Adolphus Andrews, who commanded the Eastern Sea Frontier, reported in late 1941 that he had fewer than twenty escort vessels, all of them considerably slower than a submarine sailing on the surface (as they routinely did when not in action). Andrews also possessed a few patrol planes but nowhere near the number needed to observe the eastern approaches to the United States adequately.

Interservice rivalry also contributed to the disaster. The Army Air Force possessed many planes capable of antisubmarine patrols—indeed, more than the navy had—but few airmen considered long flights over water looking for submarines to be particularly important missions. Even when they did make a sighting, the air force refused to relay its intelligence directly to local commanders, preferring instead to send the reports via official channels. As a consequence, by the time local naval forces could react, the U-boats had slipped away. A second example is the refusal of the army, which was responsible for coastal security, to impose a blackout of city lights until April 1942. Incredulous U-boat skippers often found their targets perfectly silhouetted against the bright skylines of Miami, Norfolk, New York, and dozens of other coastal cities.

Breaking the Deadlock

In late 1916, while the First World War continued its bloody stalemate on the ground, the German navy offered the kaiser a solution: Admiral von Capelle calculated that unrestricted submarine warfare in the Atlantic could sink 600,000 tons (540,000t) of shipping a month, which would starve Britain into submission within six months. Without British support, the French could not continue the war for very long. The army heartily concurred.

Several dissenting voices were raised, particularly that of German chancellor Theodor Bethmann-Hollweg. Unrestricted submarine warfare would very likely bring America into the war, he argued, with terrible consequences for Germany. The military chiefs condescendingly explained to Bethmann-Hollweg, a civilian, that the United States would take more than a year to raise an army of a million men, by which time they would have already knocked Britain and France out of the war. If, for any reason, the U-boat campaign took any longer, those million men would never be able to make it to Europe anyway, because the submarines would sink their transports en route. The kaiser approved the use of unrestricted submarine warfare on January 9, 1917, to begin on February 1.

The results are well known. As a result of the new policy, the United States declared war on Germany in April

1917. Nevertheless, for several months it looked as though the scheme might work. From February to August 1917, sinkings ran more than 500,000 tons (450,000t) a month, with a high of 875,000 tons (787,500t) in April. After that, however, the monthly average dropped well below 400,000 tons (360,000t) per month, owing to the Allied adoption of the convoy system. By June 1918, new ship construction ran more than double the tonnage sunk by submarine. Britain, though given a healthy scare, did not starve. As for American troopships, not a single one was sunk as they brought more than 2 million soldiers to France, an infusion of new blood that did indeed break the stalemate on the western front.

German U-boats, not to mention other submarines, typically scouted on the surface, then submerged to attack.

Consequently, the inhabitants of these cities were regularly treated to the spectacle of blazing tankers and freighters just a few miles offshore.

The most important blunder of the period, however, was the decision not to use convoys to shepherd maritime traffic up and down the coast. Andrews and his fellow admirals certainly recognized that convoys were the preferred solution to the submarine menace, but they calculated that large convoys with weak escorts would only serve to concentrate victims for the prowling U-boats. It would be far better, they thought, to allow ships to travel alone, using the navy's limited ASW assets to hunt for submarines along the shipping lanes. The Germans might be able to snap up single ships easily, but they would also be forced to spend the majority of their time scouting for victims. Unfortunately, the admirals miscalculated. It was the ASW corvettes and destroyers that fruitlessly swept the ocean while the canny U-boat captains worked the crowded approaches to major ports and sent freighter after freighter to the bottom of the sea.

What makes this failure particularly damning is the fact that the British had already learned the hard way that the American approach to antisubmarine warfare did not work. The Royal Navy had found during the convoy battles of 1940–1941 off its own coast that air patrols must be directly subordinated to the surface forces in the area, that weakly escorted convoys were far better than none, and that broad sweeps of the ocean by ASW task forces habitually came up empty. Moreover, the U.S. Navy had studied these battles, so it was not ignorance that prevented it from adopting tried-and-true British methods. Rather, it was bureaucratic inertia and the Anglophobia

of Admiral Ernest King, the irascible chief of naval operations.

Fighting in the manner of the Royal Navy would have required a major overhaul of the Navy Department's organization, a transformation slowed by fierce bureaucratic turf fights among the Office of Naval Intelligence, the War Plans Division, the Office of Naval Communications, and a host of other bureaus. King possessed the force of personality to overcome the resistance of deskbound sailors, but his distaste for all things British—and his conviction that American solutions would prove superior—hampered the introduction of necessary reforms.

The mounting statistics of sunken ships and drowned crews finally forced the American navy to adopt the tactics and organization of its British allies. Freighters were sinking faster than replacements could be launched from the slipways; new construction lagged behind losses by 200,000 tons (180,000t) a month, a rate that foreshadowed de-

Above: A rare sight in 1942—a German U-boat under attack from American airplanes. Below left: Although the early war policies of Admiral Ernest King turned out to be tragically misguided, he proved a quick study and ultimately swept the U-boats from the Atlantic.

feat in the Atlantic. From January to September 1942, more than half the merchantmen lost sank in American coastal waters. At the same time, U.S. ASW forces averaged only slightly more than one U-boat sinking a month. This humiliating tally ultimately resulted in a centralized and effective ASW effort: by the end of 1942, the newly formed Tenth Fleet had regained control of the eastern seaboard, and well-escorted convoys, using techniques culled largely from British experience, forced the suspension of Operation Drumbeat—nine long, bloody months after it began.

Shooting Blanks

While the German submarine fleet was sinking anything that moved along the East Coast, the American submarine fleet was simply shooting itself in the foot in the Pacific. The bulk of American submarines were, sensibly enough, deployed against the Japanese merchant marine: Japan depended on imports of raw materials from across the ocean to fuel her war industries, and her numerous Pacific outposts likewise needed a steady flow of seaborne supplies. The American submarine fleet was well trained and equipped for the job, with one notable exception: its torpedoes did not work.

Throughout the spring of 1942, U.S. submarines patrolled extensively but consistently came home empty-handed. Enraged skippers blamed the Mark XIV torpedoes, which they claimed ran deeper than programmed and thus went under, rather than into, the targets. When informed of this, the navy's Bureau of Ordnance sniffed that the submariners were merely blaming their tools for their poor shooting, and that there was nothing wrong with the Mark XIV. The demoralized submariners set up their own tests by launching torpedoes into fishing nets and measuring the resultant holes; sure enough, the torpedoes

were running 11 feet (3.3m) below their programmed depth. Unmoved, the Bureau of Ordnance rejected the tests as "unscientific." Finally, Admiral King had to intervene personally and order the Bureau to test the Mark XIV under combat conditions, something it had neglected to do. Sure enough, the Bureau sheepishly reported on August 1 that there appeared to be a problem. Six weeks later, more than nine months after Pearl Harbor, the Bureau issued a series of modifications to fix the problems found with the Mark XIV.

◆ ◆ ◆

Of course, convoys did not always work. No system is perfect, particularly when human beings must oversee it, nor is any tactic invulnerable to enemy counteraction. By mid-1942, the Germans had developed wolf-pack tactics, whereby U-boats scouted singly to cover the largest possible area of ocean, but concentrated once a convoy had been sighted to overwhelm the escorts by sheer weight of numbers. Convoys were also extremely vulnerable to air attack: they presented a large target that was difficult to provide with sufficient antiaircraft coverage. Surface raiders also posed a considerable danger, as the smaller ships normally detailed to escort duty were no match for anything larger than a light cruiser. Convoys traveling the Murmansk Run from Britain to Soviet Russia past Nazi-occupied Norway had to face all of the above dangers.

Fighting any one of these threats required constant vigilance, close coordination, and nerves of steel. Unfortunately for the seamen of one particular Murmansk convoy, the British Navy attempted to provide all three from the comfort of a command post in London.

PQ-17

Sorry to leave you like this. Good luck. Looks like a bloody business.

—Commander John Broome's last message to PQ-17

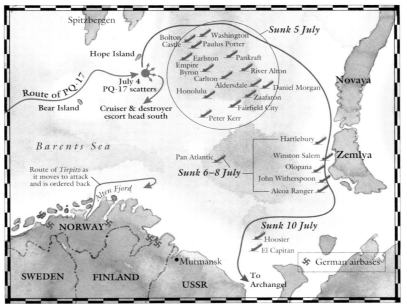

In the summer of 1942, the North Atlantic fog concealed the slow-moving freighters of convoy PQ-17. Thirty-three ships, riding low through the Arctic swell, bore nearly 180,000 tons (162,000t) of tanks, planes, ammunition, and other supplies bound for the Soviet port of Murmansk. Four cruisers and six destroyers, along with minesweepers, anti-aircraft ships, and assorted smaller craft, provided protection from German bombers, submarines, and surface warships based in occupied Norway. To the west and south, a squadron of British and American vessels, led by Admiral Sir Jack Tovey of Britain, kept a watchful eye on the Norwegian fjords for the emergence of the German battleship *Tirpitz*. The 45,000-ton (40,500t) *Tirpitz*, pride of the Nazi fleet, could make short work of PQ-17 and its escorts, should it intercept the convoy. To prevent this, Tovey's task force included the British aircraft carrier *Victorious* and two battleships.

With the German advance into the Soviet Union continuing at breakneck speed, it was vitally important for the convoy's cargo to reach its destination. The Germans had occupied the Soviets' industrial heartland the previous year, severely disrupting the production of armaments. American and British aid supplemented shortfalls in Soviet manufacturing, especially with such prosaic items as trucks, radios, and communications wire. The bulk of Western help

Top: Admiral Sir John "Jack" Tovey, commander of the squadron protecting PQ-17. Above: The Murmansk convoys typically hugged the Arctic icepack as they swung wide of German-occupied Norway before making the final dash southward to Archangel.

flowed into the Persian Gulf, and then by rail and truck through Iran and over the Caucasus Mountains into the Soviet Union. The Murmansk convoys, begun in August 1941, represented a more dangerous but more direct route.

During the short Arctic summer, ships assembled in Iceland and then hugged the polar ice cap as closely as they dared while crossing the North Atlantic and Barents Sea to Murmansk or Archangel. The summer Murmansk Run, as it came to be known, proved to be the most dangerous convoy duty of the war; subject to air, surface, or submarine attack from Norway, ships had to

sail in continuous daylight, as the sun at that time of year never set that far north. The only advantage that the merchantmen held was that heavy mists normally blanketed their movement.

But the sun shone out of a clear, blue sky on the first day of July, as PQ-17 churned along about 250 miles (400km) north of the Norwegian coast. Nervous lookouts, blinking into the dazzling northern sky, soon spotted a German scout plane, which trailed the convoy for some time. Though this plane eventually disappeared, the Germans certainly now had a fix on PQ-17's location.

During the next day, the skies remained clear, allowing German torpedo bombers to pounce. Four ships were sent to the bottom, though fortunately a heavy fog returned in the middle of the attack and forced most of the enemy planes to drop their loads blindly. The remaining freighters closed the gaps in the convoy and continued with their escorts, hoping that worsening weather might allow them to slip past the German Luftwaffe and Kriegsmarine.

Meanwhile, in London, First Sea Lord Dudley Pound agonized over a course of action. On July 4, U-boats joined the assault on PQ-17; though fended off by the hard-pressed escorts, Pound knew that the submarines would continue to stalk the convoy. They could relay the convoy's position to the *Tirpitz*, which could ravage PQ-17's escorts and the fat merchantmen almost

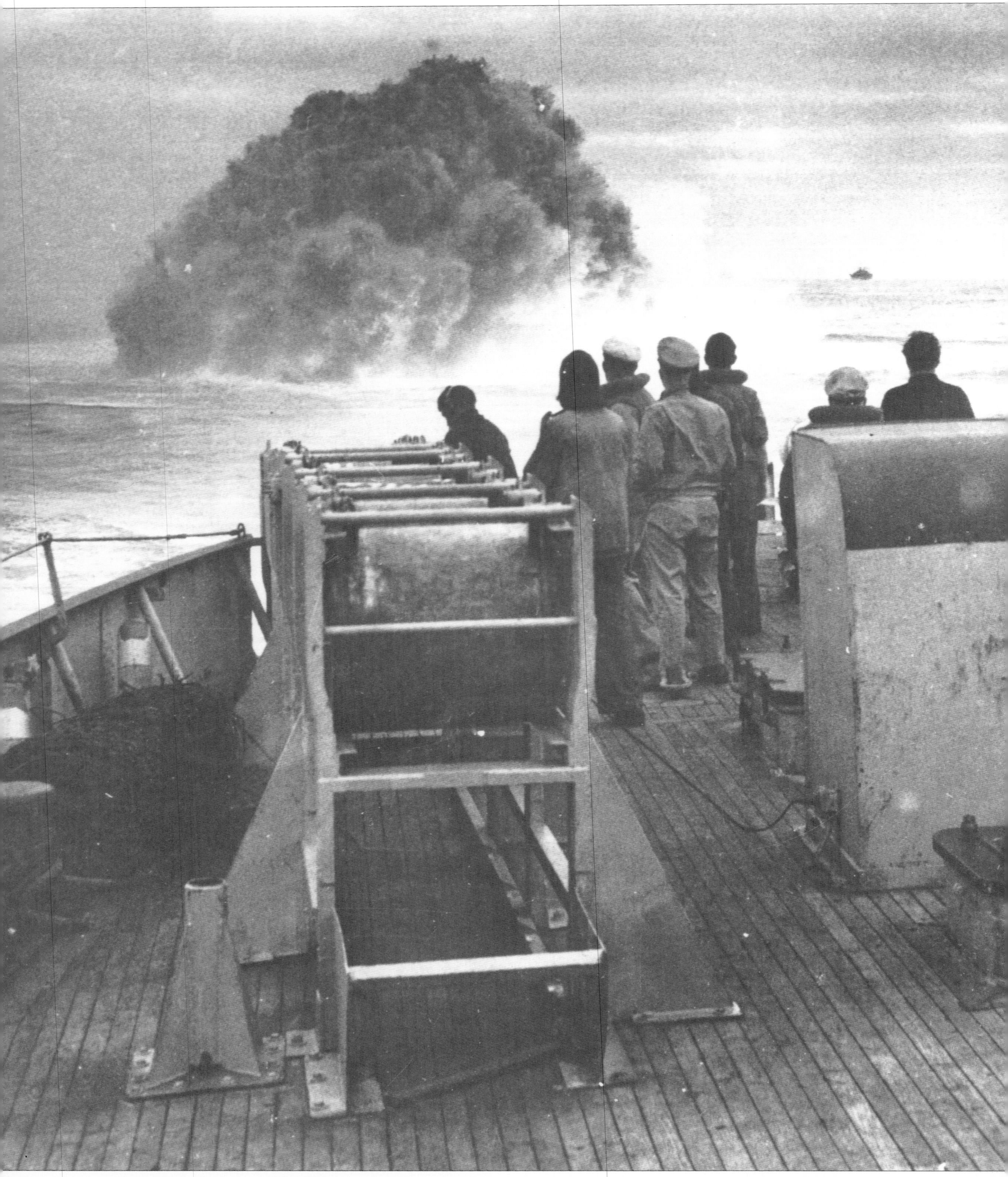

at will. With Tovey's squadron not yet in position to intervene, the only defense against the German battleship would be to scatter the convoy, which would leave the freighters at the mercy of Nazi airpower and the U-boat wolf pack. The question, then, was this: had the *Tirpitz* sailed?

So far, there were no indicators that she had. British and Russian submarines charged with maintaining watch on the Norwegian coast had not sighted her or any German destroyers, which habitually accompanied the *Tirpitz* on her sorties. Within a few days, Tovey would be in position to cover PQ-17, and the German naval high command was decidedly antsy about risking its surface fleet in the presence of enemy aircraft carriers. But Pound's nerve failed him. Late on the evening of the fourth, the admiralty sent forth a stream of signals withdrawing Tovey, ordering the cruisers to abandon the convoy and directing the freighters to disperse.

The only warships not mentioned in the dispatches were the destroyers under the command of John Broome. As he watched the escort force's heavy cruisers turn away, Broome pondered his own duty: his six ships could do little for the merchantmen once the convoy broke up; conversely, they might be of value in any confrontation with the German surface fleet. Broome concluded that the *Tirpitz* must be just over the horizon to justify the desperate measure of scattering the convoy. The destroyer commander bade the convoy farewell and hustled to join the heavier ships as they sailed west. The freighters of PQ-17 sailed on into destruction.

An escort vessel pins down a U-boat with depth charges as a convoy escapes in the background. The loss of PQ-17's destroyer escort doomed the convoy.

Ironically, the source of so much British anxiety still rode quietly at anchor. The *Tirpitz* and her accompanying flotilla did not get under way until July 5, and it returned to its sanctuary on the Norwegian coast the same day, as soon as the Kriegsmarine noted that the convoy had dispersed. Submarines and the Luftwaffe alone would deal with PQ-17.

On the fifth, the slaughter began. Waves of dive-bombers and torpedo-bombers swarmed over the virtually defenseless merchantmen, most of them armed only with light machine guns. U-boats hunted the survivors. Within hours, plumes of oily black smoke marked crippled or sinking ships; by the end of the first day, fourteen freighters had gone down. The remaining fifteen zigzagged frantically southward for the next several days, succumbing one by one. By July 9, five more ships had been sunk and a sixth had been grounded by her captain on the barren Arctic island

of Novaya Zemlya. The agony of PQ-17 ended on July 10, as the last two ships to be sunk fell victim to U-boats a mere 50 miles (80km) from landfall.

Of the thirty-five merchantmen to leave Iceland, two had been forced back by a collision early in the voyage, one had grounded, and twenty-five had been sunk by air or submarine attack. At the cost of only five aircraft, the Germans destroyed nearly 130,000 tons (117,000t) of cargo, including 400 tanks and 200 fighters. Only seven ships limped into Russian ports with their precious cargoes; four of these had saved themselves by the clever, though dangerous, tactic of entering the ice pack, painting their topsides white, and thus hiding out until the German attacks subsided. In terms of percentage of ships lost, it was the worst drubbing any convoy received throughout the war, and the disaster forced the temporary suspension of the Murmansk Run.

Opposite: Admiral Sir Dudley Pound's decision to scatter PQ-17 proved so disastrous that it has spawned numerous explanations, including various conspiracy theories. In fact, he merely took counsel of his fears. Left: A convoy of merchantmen in the North Atlantic.

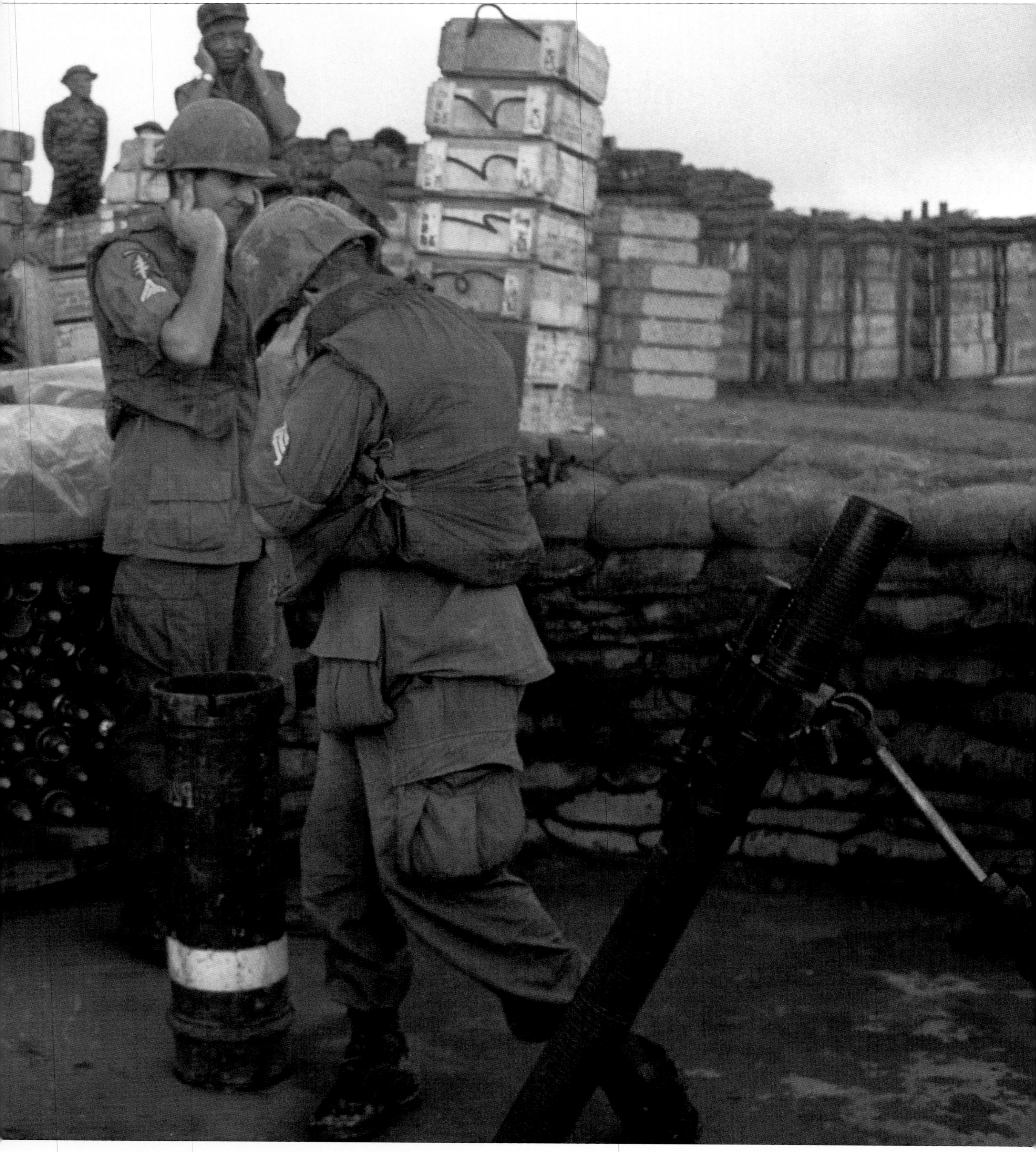

5

DIEPPE • POINTE-DU-HOE
SON TAY • DESERT ONE

Unconventional Warfare

Though war has grown phenomenally in scope, the role of specialized units paradoxically remains as important as ever, if not more so. Certainly, advances in technology have created more opportunities for the raider and more avenues for delivering commandos, saboteurs, and agents. Soldiers can be dropped out of airplanes, landed on beaches by motorized craft or submarines, or precisely inserted far behind enemy lines by helicopter. At the same time, the global scale of combat—whether during the world wars or during the Cold War—allows for unique situations that call upon the special talent of the commando.

Unconventional warfare is not easily defined, as the cases presented here will show. In general, it is the use of elite warriors trained in nonstandard techniques of combat to accomplish missions that could not easily be undertaken by regular forces. By definition, the missions are difficult and dangerous, though the rewards for success are high. The punishment for failure, conversely, is quite often the total immolation of the force.

It is almost unfair to call any failed commando mission a blunder; these missions are, after all, high-risk and therefore more prone to disaster than triumph. But certain missions have derailed not because of the inherent risks but because of some shortcoming in execution, intelligence, or planning.

The best example of this is the largest raid launched during World War II. Conceived as a dress rehearsal for the D-Day invasion, the Dieppe Raid of August 1942 involved British Royal Commandos, French and Royal Marines, Canadian infantrymen, and even a group of American Rangers. Dieppe was a port on the Pas de Calais, just across the English Channel from Great Britain. The object of the raid was to land a sizable force to seize Dieppe for a day, capture German shipping there, advance inland a short way to destroy an airfield and radar installation, and then withdraw the force. The whole affair was designed to gather data and practice techniques for the establishment of a permanent lodging in the much larger invasion that was anticipated for 1943.

Inside the Ben Het Special Forces Camp in Vietnam, these besieged Green Berets cover their ears to block out artillery fire.

Dieppe

Screams, smoke, the smell of burning cordite—mad moments soon over.

—A British commando at Dieppe

The Dieppe force departed England on the evening of August 18, 1942, and traveled across the choppy channel waters in three convoys. The easternmost convoy consisted of 3 Commando, assigned the task of destroying German batteries east of Dieppe at Berneval; 4 Commando sailed in the westernmost group, likewise tasked to silence coastal defense guns west of Dieppe at Vasterival. In the middle column were 5,000 Canadian infantry supported by thirty new Churchill tanks—commanded by Major General J. H. Roberts—and the 40 (Royal Marine) Commando.

Misfortune, a constant companion of the Dieppe raiders, arrived long before they reached the French coast. During the crossing, the eastern convoy blundered into a group of German E-boats (torpedo boats) and armed trawlers that scattered the assault craft into the night, killing and wounding many of the crews in the process. Only four of the boats ultimately reached their assigned beaches.

The other wing of the assault fared much better. Led by Lieutenant Colonel the Lord Lovat, 4 Commando stormed ashore right on schedule, just before dawn on August 19. Climbing the cliffs that backed the beaches around Dieppe, 4 Commando stormed the batteries at Vasterival, destroyed the guns with explosive charges, and then conducted a masterful fighting withdrawal to the coast. They were evacuated by mid-morning, carrying their wounded and dead off with them.

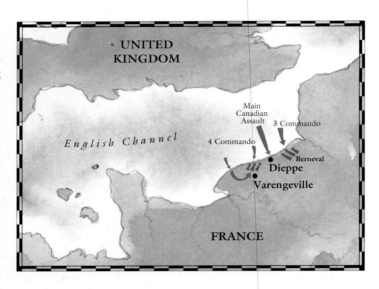

Top: Major Peter Young pulled off a considerable coup at Berneval, creating one of the few bright spots in an otherwise dark day. Above: Directly across the Channel from England, Dieppe was guarded on both flanks by heavy batteries of coastal artillery and manned by a crack garrison.

The remnants of 3 Commando washed up around Berneval. It was an eclectic group that included British seamen and commandos, French marines, and a group of American Rangers, one of whom was Lieutenant Loustalot, who would be killed at Berneval—the first American soldier to die on the European continent. With the Commando's commander drifting aboard a hulk in the channel, no one on the scene held formal authority, but the elite troops were determined to continue with their mission. Most were quickly pinned down, but one isolated platoon of eighteen men, led by Major Peter Young, gained the heights. While they were unable to take the heavy guns, their persistent efforts so distracted the crews that the Berneval

batteries played no part in the battle around Dieppe. Nearly out of ammunition, Young and his men eventually fell back to their single boat and pulled off to safety; the remainder of the Commando found their craft holed or marooned on rocks and were scooped up by the Germans.

With both wings more or less secured, the Canadians headed ashore—and into disaster. The preparatory air and naval bombardment had been an utter failure for two reasons: first, planners believed in the efficacy of a short, sharp barrage and pinned their hopes on achieving surprise rather than outright destruction of the enemy. But the Germans manning the coastal defenses had been alerted by early sightings of the invasion armada and the action around the coastal batteries, and the troops in this area were exceptionally well-drilled veterans. And second, many of the heavy guns and automatic weapons located in and around Dieppe were so well camouflaged that they had never been identified by aerial reconnaissance and thus escaped the effects of the bombardment altogether.

As a result, when the first ramps splashed down on the beach at 5:20 A.M., the defenders were ready. The invaders' smoke screen had drifted off the beach, exposing the landing craft during the last 200 yards (180m) of their approach. German guns mounted in the cliff faces blasted Allied boats full of heavily laden troops out of the water. The Churchill tanks either foundered or landed twenty minutes late, allowing the Germans to concentrate on the infantrymen who were wallowing through the surf. Well-placed machine guns worked back and forth methodically, ravaging the Canadians as they struggled forward.

Some managed to fight their way to the relative safety of the seawall or into the town itself, where they became entangled in vicious house-to-house fighting. Those who crossed to the base of the chalky cliffs were balked by thick wire barricades laced with mines and booby traps, blocking the few exits from the beach. They also discovered that the apparent security of the cliffs was in fact a death trap, as Germans above rained down satchel charges and grenades.

About a dozen or so Churchills reached shore, but beach obstacles and antitank fire kept them pinned down. Roberts had placed great faith on the Churchills' ability to carve a path through the defenses, but the tanks could do little but provide covering fire during the majority of the battle.

Subsequent waves of assault craft—those that survived the German artillery—had to nose their way past wrecked boats, abandoned tanks, and drifting bodies, the flotsam and jetsam of massacre. Reinforcements could do little but further pack the crowded beach with targets, and execution among the officers was so great that command and control on the beachhead was rapidly disintegrating. Furthermore, ammunition was beginning to run perilously low, particularly for those in Dieppe itself.

Offshore, General Roberts could not at first figure out what was happening, beyond the encouraging fact that the batteries at Berneval and Vesterival were largely silent. By midmorning, however, the scale of the disaster was becoming apparent, and before noon Roberts wisely decided to order an immediate evacuation.

This was easier said than done. The Germans had no intention of allowing the Canadians to escape, and the difficulties in merely passing the word to withdraw were nearly insurmountable. So many of the boats and assault craft

had been sunk that only a fraction of the force could be lifted at any one time. Nevertheless, through prodigies of courage on behalf of the seamen and the rear guards (most of whom were killed or captured), some of the raiders were able to regain the safety of the carrier ships and return to England.

Of the approximately 5,500 men who landed at Dieppe, more than 900 died around the little French port. Another 2,000 were made prisoners, and some 400 wounded were evacuated to England. A 60 percent casualty rate is a terrible price for any operation, and one rarely matched during a battle this brief.

German defenders clamber over an abandoned Canadian tank, one of the few that penetrated into the town itself.

The Magic Gang

Not all unconventional warfare is carried out by muscular toughs with stilettos, garrotes, and silencers—some of it doesn't even involve killing people or destroying things, at least not directly.

One example was Britain's Magic Gang, which used trickery and illusion to help defeat one of Hitler's most brilliant generals, Erwin Rommel, in North Africa. The Magic Gang built tanks and artillery from plywood and cloth, simulated tank tracks in the desert, set off charges resembling gun flashes, and hired natives to create clouds of dust with their camels—all to create the impression that an empty bit of the line actually swarmed with troops. They constructed dummy airfields to lure enemy bombers away from real ones. After a bombing raid, they dug shallow "craters" in and around the targets, spread debris on its roof, and painted in bomb damage, which led the enemy to conclude that the target had been destroyed when, in fact, it was untouched. The Gang even constructed dummy submarines from locomotive parts and empty oil drums.

The Magic Gang's greatest coup came at the Battle of El Alamein, the pivotal conflict that ended General Rommel's bid to take the Suez Canal and doomed the Axis in North Africa. They took a wrecked British scout car, doused it with blood, garlanded it with gear, dragged it out toward the German lines, and set off a charge underneath it. When the German soldiers there emerged to investigate, they came across a typical scene: a scout car, overturned by a mine and abandoned by its crew. Inside they found another of the Magic Gang's plants: a map depicting the British dispositions for the upcoming battle. Rommel was suspicious at such a propitious find, but the map was so authentic-looking—folded and torn, cribbed notes on its margins, even rings from teacups—that he eventually accepted it and based his attack partly on its bogus information.

It is unlikely that the Gang's efforts actually won the war in North Africa, but they certainly helped—and that is all unconventional warriors can ask for.

The raid against Dieppe foundered because the planners had little idea of how one went about assaulting an enemy-held coast or how hard an operation it actually was. Aside from the obvious intelligence failures and the ill-advised decision to conduct a short "surprise" barrage, the Allies learned the importance of reading tides, of coordinating assault waves, of including a great deal of engineering equipment in the lead boats, and of organizing the beachhead while under fire. Most important, they grasped the necessity of avoiding frontal attacks on enemy strong points. All these lessons, purchased with the blood and freedom of thousands of young soldiers, were put to good use two years later during the successful invasion of Normandy.

Right: Lieutenant Colonel the Lord Lovat (left) compares notes with a fellow commando after returning to England. Below: The raiders return—survivors of the Dieppe raid limp into port in Britain.

✦　✦　✦

Well, most of them were. When the Allies returned to France in June 1944, they descended on a stretch of Normandy coast that was relatively lightly defended. Landing at five separate beaches were American, British, Canadian, and Free French troops, supported by a number of special operations. Similar to the Commando mission at Dieppe, one of these operations involved seizing coastal defense guns that threatened the two American landing beaches.

The raiders who were assigned the task of destroying the big guns at Pointe-du-Hoe were better equipped and better trained than their predecessors at Dieppe, a beneficial legacy of a bloodstained debacle. And yet they failed, through no fault of their own. And unlike at Dieppe, the sacrifices were entirely useless.

Pointe-du-Hoe

Praise the Lord.

—Ranger signal from atop Pointe-du-Hoe

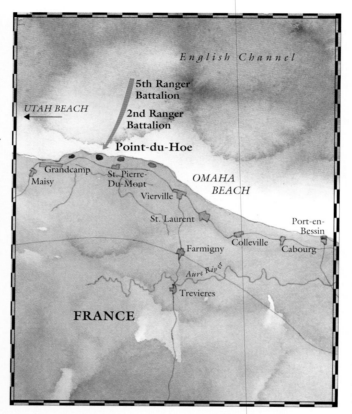

A critical adjunct to the mammoth D-Day landings was the Ranger assault at Pointe-du-Hoe, high atop cliffs overlooking the invasion beaches.

It had been a rough run inshore. Twelve Landing Craft, Assault (LCAs) had slid away from the mother ship, but two had already swamped in heavy seas, and the valiant soldiers of the 2d Ranger Battalion were bailing frantically to keep the others afloat. Lieutenant Colonel James E. Rudder, commanding from the lead LCA, peered intently at the coast of France, searching out the sheer cliffs of Pointe-du-Hoe.

The Rangers had been assigned the task of capturing the German artillery battery perched atop Pointe-du-Hoe, from which the heavy guns could range both the Omaha and Utah beaches. Emplaced in concrete-and-steel casements, the guns were well protected from naval gunfire and bombing; to protect the vulnerable troopships and landing craft as they wallowed toward shore, the guns would have to be secured by assault. Unfortunately, the beach at Pointe-du-Hoe was backed by a nearly perpendicular cliff, which was at some points 100 feet (30m) high. Machine-gun nests were situated to enfilade the beach itself, which was flat and devoid of cover.

To overcome these obstacles, the Rangers underwent training in scaling cliffs, using a variety of specialized equipment. Each LCA had mounted rocket-assisted grapnels, while four accompanying DUKWs (wheeled amphibious carriers) boasted extension ladders similar to those found on fire trucks. The

Rangers also carried lighter versions of the rocket grapnels, along with extendable ladders and rope ladders. Prior to the attack, the headland had been bombed and plastered with naval gunfire. If all went well, the Rangers would land just as the fire was lifting, fire the grappling ropes onto the cliff edge, and scramble up before the dazed defenders could react. Following them, the DUKWs would rumble across the beach and hoist up their ladders to ease the flow of reinforcements and supplies. Once atop the bluffs, each Ranger company

would use thermite grenades to destroy the German guns.

All did not go well. Rudder suddenly realized that his craft were heading for the wrong part of the coast, some three miles (4.8km) to the east of their target. Pointing this out to the British crewmen, he ordered the miniature convoy to turn right along the coast, exposing them to the fire of every strong point on the beach just a few hundred yards away. One DUKW was hit, and half the men on board were killed or wounded.

More critically, the detour cost the Rangers thirty minutes, so they touched down on dry land half an hour after the preparatory bombardment had ended. German defenders could be seen lining the cliff top, and small-arms fire began to dapple the water near the LCAs. Nevertheless, the Rangers leaped out and dashed across the 30 yards (27m) of beach to the foot of the cliffs. A few of the LCA rocket grapnels failed to lodge successfully on the cliff lip; the trailing ropes, soaked by sea spray, proved too heavy for the rockets to lift more than halfway. The DUKWs, meanwhile, could make no headway across the deeply cratered beach. Most of the grapnels shot up and hooked the top, however, and Rangers began the escalade.

The Germans cut several of the ropes, sending climbers tumbling, and dropped hand grenades down on the Rangers who were pressing against the

Above: The cliffs at Pointe-du-Hoe. Note the narrow beach and nearly vertical cliff face.
Inset: Rangers use a rope ladder to scale the heights after the action.

Bonfire of the Suicide Boats

Unconventional warfare came in many different forms. One of the oddest was the midget submarine, a weapon developed by nearly every participant in World War II. Equipped with a crew of one to four men, these submarines were used for exceedingly dangerous underwater work, usually involving attacks on enemy shipping in their ports or along their home coasts. Casualty rates among the crews of midget subs were so high that the vessels were commonly referred to as suicide boats.

In one case, many of these brave crews weren't given the opportunity to give their lives for their fatherland, perhaps to their secret relief. The German navy, reduced to desperation in the latter stages of the war, had built hundreds of Biber ("beaver" in German) midget submarines. These one-man subs carried two torpedoes and typically stalked freighters along the mainland coast of the English Channel. Only one in three survived any given mission.

In January 1945, a flotilla of thirty Bibers was being readied for a sortie to the Scheldt estuary when a mechanic inadvertently fired a torpedo into the closely packed mass. The boats exploded in a chain reaction, sending the Bibers to the bottom but giving their pilots a renewed lease on life.

James E. Rudder, one of the "founding fathers" of the Rangers, was a former football star (at Texas A&M) and a highly decorated infantryman. Here, he is shown later in the war.

cliff. Machine guns lashed the beach continuously; within a few minutes, fifteen Rangers had become casualties.

Coming to the rescue were two destroyers, the British *Talybont* and the American *Satterlee*. Cruising dangerously close to shore, they smothered the defenders with main battery and machine-gun fire and drove them back from the cliff's edge. Granted a respite, the Rangers used the remaining ropes and their own ingenuity to scale Pointe-du-Hoe; one group cut footholds at the top of their 16-foot (4.8m) scaling ladder, hauled the ladder up and held it while others climbed past them, then repeated the process. In this manner, as individuals or squads, the Rangers secured the cliff top thirty minutes after landing and immediately swept forward toward the gun emplacements.

The plateau was blasted and torn by shellfire, but most of the defenders had retreated to avoid fighting the Rangers on more equal terms. One by one, the emplacements fell into American hands, but neither Rudder nor his men felt able to rejoice. Every single casement was empty—the heavy guns had been evacuated long before D-Day. All the effort, the sacrifice of elite soldiers (almost forty of 225 put out of action), and the months of training had come to naught because of a failure to recognize that the target was simply no longer there.

◆ ◆ ◆

One of the best-executed unconventional operations in history took place during the Vietnam War, a conflict marked by its reliance on special forces. Complex, dangerous, and poised precariously between success and disaster, the Son Tay raid typified both the endlessly rehearsed drills and the spontaneous initiative that characterize unconventional warfare. But like the Rangers' ascent of Pointe-du-Hoe, it was a failure.

Convoys of landing craft churn toward the Norman coast. The invasion was a success—but not as a result of the sacrifice of the Rangers at Pointe-du-Hoe.

Son Tay

In retrospect, it might appear that excessive forces and resources were committed to the operation.

—Son Tay after-action report

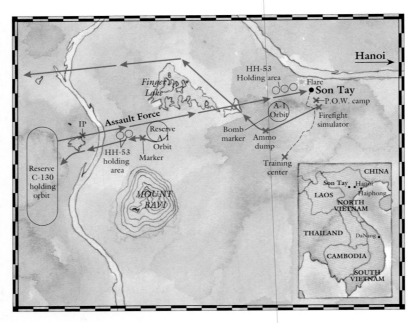

I in the wee hours of November 21, 1970, the grumbling pilots of three American aircraft carriers catapulted their craft into the night air of the Tonkin Gulf. They were slated to fly their A-7 attack planes and F-8 fighter escorts over North Vietnam, into the heart of the densest air defenses in the world around Haiphong harbor—without bombs. Political restrictions forbade them from actually attacking the north, so they were to penetrate North Vietnamese airspace, stir up the hornet's nest, and dispense flares before returning to their carriers. The fliers had no idea why they were doing this, other than to provide a distraction for some unknown special operation. Typical Vietnam ridiculousness, they thought.

Unbeknownst to these fliers, the operation that they were supporting was an effort to liberate seventy American prisoners who were believed to be held at a small outpost some 24 miles (38.4km) west of Hanoi. As North Vietnamese MiGs rose to meet the navy planes, five American HH-53 helicopters roared in across the flat agricultural scrubland that surrounded Son Tay, the only known prison camp outside the North Vietnamese capital. The helicopters had lifted off from the Royal Thai Air Force Base at Udorn, refueled from modified C-130 tankers, and flown across Laos and the rugged highlands that marked North Vietnam's boundary.

Top: Colonel Arthur Simons, leader of the Son Tay raid, at a press conference after the mission. Above: The raid to rescue prisoners of war at Son Tay was arguably the best executed American special operation in history—and a complete bust.

Inside the helicopters were hand-picked soldiers from a number of elite organizations: Green Berets of the 6th and 7th Special Forces Groups and the air force's top chopper crews from the Aerospace Rescue and Recovery Service. Trundling nearby were C-130 Combat Talon planes, operated by the 7th Special Operations Squadron and the 1st Special Operations Wing, while air force fighters, ground attack planes, and F-105 Wild Weasel electronic warfare aircraft circled protectively overhead. All told, including the navy's diversion, 105 aircraft converged over North Vietnam that night.

Colonel Arthur D. "Bull" Simons, flying in one of the HH-53s, led the

raid. The army's premier unconventional warrior, he had been largely responsible for putting together the team and had driven them through months of training in Florida, using a full-scale mock-up of Son Tay for dress rehearsals. Every possible contingency had been identified and planned for during the exercises, which included 170 run-throughs by Simons's own count. Security had been so tight that the soldiers did not know who they were supposed to rescue or where the raid was actually to take place until the night before, when the force had already gathered in Thailand.

Two HH-53s, spares for the mission, hung back while a third pulled away from the group and eased into a firing position just over the camp. Miles away, a C-130 was dropping firefight simulators (fireworks designed to replicate the look and sound of a small-arms skirmish) to distract North Vietnamese troops in the area. Another C-130 began to drop flares, lighting up the entire area just before twin Gatling guns that were mounted in the HH-53 spewed 4,000 rounds per minute into the camp's guard towers and barracks. With these reduced to sawdust, the gunship moved off to a landing area.

Coming in behind it was a smaller HH-3 helicopter carrying a thirteen-man assault team. There was no open area inside the walls large enough to land a helicopter safely, so Simons came up with a simple, if dangerous, solution:

the HH-3 purposefully crash-landed, its blades striking the trees that guarded the best available spot; the controlled crash was handled with such aplomb by the pilot that not one member of the assault team was injured, and the soldiers tumbled out inside the compound. While one man used a bullhorn to urge the prisoners to stay down, the rest of the team mowed down the few stunned North Vietnamese who were stumbling around the camp.

Just outside the prison, a fourth HH-53 dropped its assault team. This group blew a hole in the camp wall, through which the prisoners were to be evacuated, and then proceeded to clear and demolish various outbuildings.

The only glitch in the plan coincidentally turned out to be one of its most fortunate elements. A small group of buildings, thought to be a secondary school, lay just south of Son Tay. Its similarity to the prison camp had been noted during training, and special warnings were issued to the pilots not to mistake it for the target. But the helicopter

ferrying Simons and half the Green Berets landed there anyway, the pilot slightly disoriented after the long flight from Thailand in the darkness.

Simons recognized the error instantly, but there was little he could do about it, as he suddenly found himself engaged by hundreds of enemy troops. Not one to hang back, Simons ordered his men to assault the "school," which they did with admirable efficiency. Within ten minutes of landing, the raiders had killed 100 to 200 heavily armed enemy troops, reduced the compound to a blazing ruin, and lifted off to rejoin the main action at Son Tay, all without sustaining a single casualty. The pilot's blunder might have saved the entire force—Simons had just annihilated, albeit inadvertently, the one enemy element that could have effectively interfered, just a few football fields' distance away from the prison camp. (As it turned out, most of the soldiers at the "school" were either Chinese or Russian advisers stationed in North Vietnam to train their communist brethren, a

A C-130, similar to those employed in the Son Tay raid, flies over Southeast Asia.

Blunting the Tool

If you use a screwdriver as a chisel, it eventually becomes useless for its designated purpose. Similarly, the misuse of Special Forces has been a recurring theme throughout their history, a blunder committed by commanders who consider them a sort of super-infantry (which they are) and not the relatively fragile specialists that they were meant to be. Two of the worst examples of this way of thinking occurred during World War II and in Vietnam.

The Rangers were conceived as a force for raids or assaults that require specialized training in demolition, climbing, night operation, and the like. But during the long fight across North Africa and up the Italian boot from 1942 to 1944, generals could not resist putting the Rangers into the line. The Rangers invariably fought well, but the steady casualties and the necessity of accepting replacements without the requisite skills of true Rangers eroded the quality of the Ranger battalions. This misuse of elite soldiers culminated in disaster at Cisterna, Italy. Spearheading an Allied attack, three Ranger battalions pushed ahead too quickly for supporting units to keep up with them, and they ran into a nest of tough German paratroopers and accompanying panzers. Only eighteen men from the 1st and 3rd Ranger Battalions escaped death or capture, while the 4th Ranger Battalion suffered 180 casualties.

Likewise, Special Forces units in Vietnam (better known as the Green Berets) were supposed to operate clandestinely behind enemy lines, training indigenous troops for self-defense and conducting various kinds of missions, among them long-range reconnaissance and sabotage missions such as seizing or assassinating key communist political or military leaders. The Green Berets were linguists, medics, demolition experts, communications specialists, and politicians, expected to possess a high degree of independent judgment and initiative. But short-sighted commanders frequently tied the Special Forces groups to isolated fire bases deep in enemy territory, where they became ready, if difficult, targets for Viet Cong attacks. In several cases, these Special Forces camps were overrun—though typically at high cost—resulting in the loss at a single blow of dozens of these highly trained unconventional warriors.

fact hushed up after the raid so as not to offend Hanoi's patrons.)

Back at Son Tay, Simons landed in time to help mop up around the compound and turn back a few tentative enemy probes from the perimeter. He also suffered a devastating blow—his subordinates reported that the compound was empty. Not a single prisoner was present. There was little time for mourning, however; Simons hustled his raiders back onto the helicopters while a demolitions expert set a charge in the wrecked HH-3. The explosion flared as the HH-53s disappeared into the darkness, noses turned toward Thailand.

✦ ✦ ✦

It had been perfect, really. One slightly wounded Green Beret and a crew chief with a broken ankle were the only casualties during an operation that had penetrated into the enemy heartland, destroyed two military installations, and killed or wounded more than 200 communist troops. The failure, as at Pointe-du-Hoe, stemmed from not realizing that the true target had moved. Unlike in the Normandy operation, however, planners had known that they were probably attacking a dry hole. Last-minute intelligence reports, from spies in Hanoi and from infrared photography, made it reasonably certain that the POWs were no longer at Son Tay. But six months of planning and training had its own momentum; it seemed almost criminal to call off the raid on the eve of its departure. More important, the decision makers from the president on down wanted the prisoners to be there so badly that they blinded themselves to the weight of evidence, as if wishful thinking might make the unlikely real.

Because the raid went so well, those responsible for evaluating the available

A model of the Son Tay camp used during training for the assault force. Note the small courtyard where the HH-3 helicopter crash-landed.

intelligence data were never really called to task for their mistakes. A decade later, a similar operation did end in flaming ruin. This time, though, it was not the intelligence officers who were at fault. If Son Tay proved that meticulous planning can be undone by weak intelligence, the Iranian hostage rescue demonstrated that poor planning readily undoes itself.

Desert One

I said, "My God, I am going to fail."

—Colonel Charlie Beckwith

The overly complex American plan to rescue U.S. hostages in Iran called for no less than four covert rendezvous and a risky assault in the streets of Teheran.

By April 1980, the fifty-three Americans who had been seized by Iranian radicals in Tehran had languished in captivity for nearly five months. During that time, at bases in Arizona and North Carolina, soldiers, sailors, airmen, and marines had been rehearsing a rather complicated rescue plan: Rangers, Delta Force commandos, and Green Berets were scheduled to fly from an island off the coast of Oman to a remote desert site 265 miles (424km) from Tehran. There they would rendezvous with eight helicopters to be launched from an American aircraft carrier in the Gulf of Oman. The Green Berets would then board the helicopters and fly to another location, this time in the mountains east of Tehran, where they would conceal the helicopters and lie low until dark. Climbing aboard vans and trucks supplied by local agents, the raiders would drive into Tehran and storm the American Embassy and the nearby Iranian Ministry of Foreign Affairs, thereby freeing the hostages. The rescuers and their charges would then be picked up by the helicopters and flown to still another locale, a deserted airstrip to the southeast. At this airstrip, secured by Rangers flown in from Egypt, the whole force would be transferred to transport planes and evacuated. The helicopters, too short-ranged to escape, would be destroyed.

During the evening of April 24, 1980, six C-130 transports took off from Masirah Island, carrying American Rangers, Iranian translators, and members of Delta Force, America's secretive antiterrorist unit. The Deltas wore civilian clothes underneath their military gear and flak vests in order to facilitate escape if the mission went awry. Also on board was Colonel Charlie Beckwith, commander of the assault team. Beckwith, a veteran of Korea and three tours in Vietnam as a Green Beret, had assumed the mantle once worn by Bull Simons as America's premier unconventional warrior. The plain-spoken Beckwith had already voiced his dissatisfaction with the plan to his superiors, but like a good soldier he stifled those objections once the operation was under way.

The subjects of one of Beckwith's complaints were simultaneously rising from the flight deck of the USS *Nimitz*, on station in the Gulf of Oman. Eight Sea Stallion helicopters sped across the gulf waters and into southern Iran. Beckwith had argued vehemently that since he needed at least six operable helicopters to accomplish the mission, more than eight should be dispatched to allow for breakdowns. His request was turned down, however, for reasons that have yet to be made clear.

All went well for the Sea Stallions as they churned across Iran in tight formation, but a formidable obstacle lay ahead. Weather forecasters had predicted the possible billowing up of a haboob, a huge dust cloud not uncommon to the high Iranian desert. Unfortunately for the marine pilots, security precautions prevented the weather warning from being transmitted to them before the flight; in fact, they had never been briefed on or trained for the possibility of having to fly through a milky—and seemingly endless—cloud of dust that was the consistency of talcum powder. Now, only a few hours after taking off, the Sea Stallions entered the haboob.

Flying on instrument guidance alone and forbidden to talk to one an-

Above: President Jimmy Carter briefs House and Senate leaders on the failed rescue mission. Left: Colonel Charlie Beckwith opposed the rescue plan, but he did his best to carry it out.

other over the radio for fear that the Iranians might detect their transmissions, the helicopters quickly became separated. One Sea Stallion was forced down by a blade problem; spotted by another craft, the crew abandoned its helicopter and flew on to Desert One with the others. Another Sea Stallion suffered the breakdown of a cooling motor, which led to erratic control and the loss of the instrumentation necessary to fly in the haboob. If the pilot could have contacted the other helicopters in the flight, he might have discovered that he was only minutes away from breaking into the clear air and perhaps would have risked continuing on; unwilling to break radio silence, however, he did not know how close he was, and he aborted on his own initiative, returning to the *Nimitz*. The rescue mission was now down to the bare minimum of six helicopters.

At Desert One, Beckwith waited impatiently, everything in readiness. His team had landed by 10 P.M., the first two C-130s departing and the remainder carrying fuel for the approaching helicopters. Rangers had erected roadblocks around the area, already capturing a bus of forty-four mystified Iranians, whom Beckwith planned on flying out in a C-130 as soon as refueling was complete.

Iranian soldiers, newsmen, and clerics survey the site at Desert One.

Finally, the first Sea Stallion arrived, followed by five stragglers over the next ninety minutes.

The night was rapidly slipping away, but concerns about losing the cover of darkness faded when a third helicopter reported mechanical difficulties, this time a leaky hydraulic system. Beckwith immediately recommended that the mission be scrubbed; as he had foreseen, eight Sea Stallions were not enough.

While Beckwith's bad news traveled at the speed of light through several layers of command all the way to the Oval Office of President Jimmy Carter, Colonel James Kyle ordered the helicopters to re-fuel for the flight back to the *Nimitz*. Kyle commanded the transport aircraft and was responsible for all aerial activity at Desert One, which, at that moment, was growing increasingly chaotic. One of the great shortcomings of the training program was that the entire force had never actually practiced this portion of the plan, possibly the most ticklish element short of the actual rescue.

The four C-130s and five helicopters all kept their engines running, creating a hellish roar and great clouds of dust. These elements, combined with the pitch-blackness and the fact that many of the principals had never met

one another, made it difficult to recognize individuals involved in the mission. As a result, no one maintained effective control of the refueling, and the inevitable happened: a Sea Stallion maneuvering toward the fuelers suddenly banked right, crashing into a C-130 packed with troops, ammunition, and aviation fuel. Both craft exploded, incinerating eight crewmen and sending the survivors scrambling from the burning hulks. The C-130 continued to rock as the ammunition caught fire, and Kyle instantly ordered Desert One evacuated, fearful that the remaining transports might suffer damage. Frantic crews jettisoned weapons, vehicles, and other gear to make room for passengers; the helicopter crewmen wanted to blow their Sea Stallions in place, but Kyle forbade it. His only concern was to salvage what he could from the conflagration. Within a half hour of the crash, the three C-130s departed Desert One, leaving behind five perfectly good helicopters, mounds of equipment, some very confused Iranians, and the bodies of eight comrades.

Desert One was a disaster in many ways: it was a desperate gamble that cut too many corners and relied too much on good fortune. Despite months of preparation and (for once) accurate intelligence, there were many unanticipated problems, such as the haboob, the mechanical breakdowns, and the difficulty in refueling at a crowded, dark, noisy airstrip in the middle of nowhere. The failure dealt a heavy blow to the prestige of American arms; cost eight lives, one C-130 transport, and seven helicopters —all self-inflicted losses; and caused the hostages to be dispersed throughout Iran to prevent another such attempt. The Iranians also recovered secret documents in the abandoned Sea Stallions

The charred wreckage of Desert One. Two bodies lay in the foreground, left in place by the Iranians for the edification of the world media.

that identified safe houses, radio frequencies, and codes used by local agents, many of whom undoubtedly died as a result. The only bright spot, if it can be called such, was that the early abort of the mission probably saved lives in the long run. If the ill-favored rescue attempt had continued, odds are that most of the raiders would have perished in the twisted streets of Tehran.

Conclusion

Those of you who have read both my books on military blunders have seen how the nature of war (and of the blunders themselves) has changed over the course of two millennia. Even those who have read only the present volume, however, should have discerned several common themes. First, war is a messy, exhausting, and frustrating business—and an unforgiving one as well. The great Napoleon once said that the victorious general is he who has made the fewest mistakes. Therefore, one should try to reserve some sympathy for the blunderer and to understand that failure in war does not automatically equate with failure of intelligence or some moral defect. Mistakes or failures on the battlefield are often (perhaps typically) the result of a commander's inability to deal with pressures rarely experienced in other fields.

Second, blunders often stem from a lack of what fighter pilots call "situational awareness" (that is, keeping track of the relative positions of friends and foes in a rapidly shifting dogfight). Commanders must retain a feel for the enemy's capabilities and intentions, understand the strengths and weaknesses of their own forces, and correctly perceive the effects of weather and terrain on both. Even for the modern general, supported by a huge staff, this can be a difficult task. Moreover, we see again and again how preconceived notions and fond expectations cause commanders to lose touch with reality, as in the case of Hitler's invasion of Russia or the American war effort in Vietnam. I have often suspected that Hitler's retreat from reality, for instance, originated in the inadmissible (even to himself) realization that the war was truly lost.

Third, the tools of war are advancing far more rapidly now than in the past. During this century, each new generation of officers faced a transformed battlefield. In the coming century, change may occur even more frenetically, widening the scope for errors of preparation and execution. Warfare is also extending itself, however tentatively, into space, just as it expanded into the air over the past eighty years, offering a new battleground for the military blunderer.

Finally, the sheer complexity and scope of modern warfare is making it increasingly difficult to assign blame for disaster. Commanders must rely on technology they do not completely understand, on swollen staffs of specialists in communications, logistics, and intelligence, and on the restraint of political leaders who now have the ability to interfere with operations at the speed of light. Of course, intelligent men and women in the armed services are wrestling with these problems today, and solutions to them will undoubtedly be found, for humanity has a peculiar genius for war.

Nevertheless, I believe that, 100 years from now, some author still unborn will be able to write a companion volume to this book. May God protect the soldiers and sailors whose tales fill its chapters.

These three photographs capture the major changes in warfare during this century: the bureaucratization, mechanization, and industrialization of human conflict.

Bibliography

Appleman, Roy. *East of Chosin*. College Station, Tex.: Texas A&M University Press, 1987.

Asprey, Robert. *War in the Shadows*. Garden City, N.Y.: Doubleday & Company, Inc., 1975.

Blair, Clay, Jr. *Silent Victory*. New York: J.B. Lippincott Company, 1975.

Chew, Allen. *Fighting the Russians in Winter: Three Case Studies*. Fort Leavenworth, Kans.: U.S. Army Command and General Staff College, 1981.

Cohen, Eliot, and John Gooch. *Military Misfortunes*. New York: The Free Press, 1990.

Condon, Richard. *The Winter War: Russia Against Finland*. New York: Ballantine Books, 1971.

Fair, Charles. *From the Jaws of Victory*. New York: Simon & Schuster, 1971.

Fall, Bernard. *Hell in a Very Small Place*. New York: Da Capo Press, Inc., 1966.

Ghinnery, Phil. *Air War in Vietnam*. New York: Exeter Books.

Harris, Walter. *France, Spain and the Rif*. New York: Longmans, Green & Co., 1927.

Historical Division, War Department. *Small Unit Actions*. Washington, D.C.: U.S. Government Printing Office, 1947.

Hopkins, William. *One Bugle, No Drums*. Chapel Hill, N.C.: Algonquin Books of Chapel Hill, 1986.

Jablonski, Edward. *Airwar*. Garden City, N.Y.: Doubleday & Company, Inc., 1971.

Ladd, James. *Commandos and Rangers of World War II*. New York: St Martin's Press, 1978.

McNamara, Robert, with Brian VanDeMark. *In Retrospect*. New York: Times Books, 1995.

Mason, Herbert, Jr. *The Commandos*. New York: Meredith Press, 1966.

Mellor, F.H. *Morocco Awakes*. London: Methuen Publishers, 1939.

Mossman, Billy. *Ebb and Flow: November 1950–July 1951*. Washington, D.C.: Center of Military History, 1990.

Oberdorfer, Don. *Tet!* Garden City, N.Y.: Doubleday & Company, 1971.

O'Neill, Richard. *Suicide Squads*. London: Salamander Books, 1981.

Pisor, Robert. *The End of the Line*. New York: W.W. Norton, 1982.

Regan, Geoffrey. *Great Military Disasters*. New York: M. Evans & Company, 1987.

Reit, Seymour. *Masquerade: The Amazing Camouflage Deceptions of World War II*. New York: Hawthorn Books, 1978.

Ryan, Paul. *The Iranian Rescue Mission*. Annapolis, Md.: United States Naval Institute, 1985.

Schemmer, Benjamin. *The Raid*. New York: Harper & Row, 1980.

Sowden, William. *The Victory at Sea*. Garden City, N.Y.: Doubleday, Page & Company, 1920.

Stanton, Shelby. *America's Tenth Legion*. Novato, Calif.: Presidio, 1989.

Warner, Denis, and Peggy Warner. *The Tide at Sunrise*. New York: Charterhouse, 1974.

Index

M

N

O

P

Pakistan, 50
Panjshir Valley (Afghanistan), 49–51
Panzers, 7, 11, 18, 19
Paukenschlag, 85–88
Paulus, Colonel-General Friedrich, 19, 23
Pearl Harbor, 61, 81
Persamo (Finland), 11
Philippines, 36, 61
Piroth, Colonel Charles, 39, 40
Ploesti, 9, 60–64
Pointe-du-Hoe (France), 9, 100–103
Poland, 11
Pound, First Sea Lord Dudley, 89, 91, *92*, 93
P'yongyang (Korea), 26

R

Raate (Finland), 12
Radar, 54, 56
Rafid Gap, 30
Ridgway, General Matthew, 29
Rif tribe, 36–38
Roberts, Major General J.H., 96, 97
Rolling Thunder, 8, 70–73
Romania, 60
Rostow, Walter, 70
Rozhdestvenski, Rear Admiral Zinovi, 76, 77, 78, 80, 81
Rudder, Lieutenant James E., 100, *102*, 103
Russia, 18–23, 75
Russian military units
  163rd Rifle Division, 12, 14, 15
  Ninth Army, 11
  Second Pacific Squadron, 76
  Third Pacific Squadron, 76, 77
Russo-Finnish War, 16

S

Sabotage, 46, 106
Saigon (Vietnam), 44, 45, 46
Saint Petersburg (Russia), 76
Salang Tunnel (Afghanistan), 49, 51
Satterlee (destroyer), 103
Schweinfurt (Germany), 9
Sea of Japan, 76, 77
Shanghai, 76, 77
Ships
  Agaki (aircraft carrier), 82
  Alexander III (battleship), 79, 80
  Almaz (cruiser), 76
  Anti-Submarine Warfare ships, 85, 87
  Borodino (battleship), 78, 79, *78–79*, 80
  E-boats, 96
  Enterprise (carrier), 84
  Hiryu (carrier), 82, 84
  Hornet (battleship), *74*, 75
  Izumi (cruiser), 78
  Kaga (carrier), 82, 84
  Landing Craft Assaults, 100
  Nimitz (carrier), 108, 109, 110
  Oslyabya (battleship), 79
  Satterlee (destroyer), 103
  Soryu (carrier), 82, 84
  Suvarov (battleship), 78, 79, 80
  Talybone (destroyer), 103
  Tirpitz (battleship), 89, 91, 92
  U-boats, 85, 86, *86*, 87, *87*, 88, 92, 93
  Victorious (carrier), 89
  wheeled amphibious carriers, 100
  Yorktown (carier), 83, *83*, 84, *84*
Siilasvuo, Colonel Hjalmar, 12, 14, 15, 16
Silvestre, General Manuel, 36–38
Simons, Colonel Arthur, 104, *104*, 107, 108
Singapore, 77
Six Day War, 11, 30
Son Tay (Vietnam), 9, 104–107
Soryu (carrier), 82, 84
Soviet Union. *See* Russia.
Spanish-American War, 36

Stalingrad (Russia), 9, 18–23
Submarines, 75, 89
  midget, 102
  in World War I, 86
  in World War II, 85–88, 92, 102
Suez Canal, 76, 98
Suomussalmi (Finland), 9, 12–17
Supplies, 11, 18, 19, 23, 36, 39, 41, 42, 48, 50, 56
Suvarov (battleship), 78, 79, 80
Syria, 30

T

Talybone (destroyer), 103
Tanks, 11
  Churchill, 96, 97
  Elefant, 22
  Panther, 22
Tank traps, 7
Taylor, Maxwell, 70
Tehran (Iran), 108
Tet Offensive, 8, 43–48
Thailand, 70
Tirpitz (battleship), 89, 91, 92
Togo, Admiral Heihachiro, 77, 78, *78*, 79, *81*
Tonkin Gulf (Vietnam), 104
Tourkmani, Colonel Hassan, 30–31, 33
Tovey, Admiral Sir John, 89, *89*, 91
Tsugaru Strait (Japan), 76, 77
Tsushima Strait (Japan), 76–81
Turkey, 64

U

Ualu river, 26
Utah beach (France), 100

V

Vasterival (France), 96
Victorious (carrier), 89
Viet Cong, 43, 44, 46
Viet Minh, 39, 40, *40*, 42

W

Y

Z

Photography Credits

AP/Wide World Photos: pp. 22, 27, 44, 61, 66, 89, 90, 92, 93, 102 bottom

Archive Photos: pp. 9 top, 21, 28, 34, 49 top left, 59, 74, 82, 99, 104 top, 113 top; © A.F.P.: pp. 32, 39 top left; © Imapress/S. Herbert: p. 51; © Popperfoto: p. 52; © Express Newspapers: p. 112

Brown Brothers: pp. 77, 83, 86 top, 103

Corbis-Bettmann: pp. 36 top left, 62, 80, 85 top right, 109 bottom

Hulton Deutsch Collection Limited: pp. 18 top left, 19, 20, 38, 55, 56, 58, 67 both, 76 top, 78, 79, 81, 97, 99 bottom, 101 background

E.T. Archive: Charles Cundall, *The Withdrawal from Dunkirk June 1940*: p. 2

National Archives: p. 88

Reuters/Corbis-Bettmann: pp. 31, 50

All maps by Steven Stankiewicz

Underwood Photo Archives: pp. 66, 86 bottom

UPI/Corbis-Bettmann: pp. 6, 8, 9 bottom, 10, 13 both, 14, 15, 17, 23, 24, 33, 37, 40, 41, 42, 43 top, 45 both, 46, 47, 48, 57, 60 top right, 64 both, 68, 69, 71, 72, 73, 84, 87 both, 94, 96 top left, 99 top, 101 inset, 102 top, 105, 106, 107, 109 top, 110, 111, 113 bottom